They took my
father

They took my father

A STORY OF IDEALISM AND BETRAYAL

MAYME SEVANDER

WITH
LAURIE HERTZEL

 Pfeifer-Hamilton

Pfeifer-Hamilton, Publisher
1702 E Jefferson St
Duluth MN 55812
(218) 728-6807

They Took My Father

Printed in the United States of America
by Versa Press Inc

10 9 8 7 6 5 4 3 2 1

The research and writing for this book were made possible, in part, by
the generous support of the College of St. Scholastica, Duluth, Minnesota.

Editorial Director: Susan Gustafson
Assistant Editor: Patrick Gross
Art Director: Joy Morgan Dey
Editorial Consultant: Tom Morgan

Library of Congress Cataloging in Publication Data
92-80225

ISBN 0-938586-64-5

Dedicated to the memory of my beloved parents,
Oscar and Katri Corgan,

and to the other North American Finns
whose search for equality and opportunity
led them to Soviet Russia,
where their ideals were ultimately betrayed

Contents

NORWAY

SWEDEN

FINLAND

Murmansk

Kandalaksha

White Sea

Uhtua
Kem
Latushka
Bielomorsk

KARELIA

Archangel

Medvezh'yegorsk

Kondopoga
Lake Onega

Petrozavodsk

Gulf of Bothnia

Baltic Sea

Lake Ladoga

Helsinki

Gulf of Finland

Leningrad

ESTONIA

Vologda

Tcherepovets

LATVIA

LITHUANIA

UNION
OF SOVIET
SOCIALIST
REPUBLICS

Moscow

Statute miles 0   50   100   150   200   250

Foreword

On a damp, chilly morning in 1986, a train carrying thirty-three Duluthians pulled into Petrozavodsk station in what was then the Soviet Union. Our group had been planning this trip for months, and we were amazed and excited finally to be here. Mikhail Gorbachev had been in power only a short time, and the Cold War was not yet over. It was still unusual for Americans to travel to the Soviet Union, especially to cities like this one that were small and off the beaten track.

We had made this long trip in order to forge sister city ties between our hometown of Duluth, Minnesota, and this strange city in the north of Russia, but we had no idea if our venture would be successful. No one in Petrozavodsk had responded to our repeated letters and telexes, so we finally just bought plane tickets and came over. Now, as we waited for the train to shudder to a stop, we wondered if there would be anyone there to meet us.

Little did we know that the most amazing part of our journey was waiting for us there on the platform.

As we stepped off the train, a group of Petrozavodsk citizens holding flowers and umbrellas surged forward to greet us. "Welcome to Russia!" someone said in clear English. "Hello, Duluth!"

The people waiting for us in the rain were once Americans, many of them former Minnesotans and Wisconsinites who had moved to Russia fifty years before, as children, and who had grown up under Stalin. Most had lost touch with American friends and relatives. Our arrival represented, to them, the first chance of renewing those ties.

Making Duluth and Petrozavodsk formal sister cities suddenly seemed almost redundant. We had been related for half a century; we just hadn't known it.

The quest to find a sister city in Russia had begun years earlier, with Brooks Anderson and Ron Caple of Duluth.

Many people were skeptical that such a relationship would be possible. McCarthyism and the Cold War had built a wall of suspicion between our two countries. But in the spring of 1986, a group of thirty-three volunteers gathered around Brooks and Ron, and plans were under way.

The selection of Petrozavodsk was pure luck. Brooks had been looking for a city that matched Duluth, and Petrozavodsk, the capital of Soviet Karelia, seemed a natural. The city is located near the Finnish border, and, like Duluth, it has a sizable Finnish population. It is an inland port on a large northern lake, and is surrounded by dense forests dotted with smaller lakes. Mining, logging, tourism and papermaking are the principal industries.

But that was all we knew. We didn't know that, back in the 1930s, Petrozavodsk had been settled by several thousand American and Canadian Finns, many from the Midwest—many from Northern Minnesota.

Half a century and half a world had separated us, and the reunion in 1986 was overwhelming. It was a visit many of the Soviets had waited nearly a lifetime for, a visit most of the Americans found amazing and fortuitous almost beyond belief. During that first four-day trip to Petrozavodsk, we were pressed with questions about life in the states, and we responded with dozens of questions of our own. How had this happened, this mass exodus? How many people had actually emigrated from our Northland? And why didn't most of us Americans know anything about this historical connection between our two cities?

As the story unfolded, I realized I felt a sense of anger—anger that I could have been reared and educated in Duluth and yet be ignorant of this important chapter in the history of my community. And I wanted to make sure that this story would be told.

In the years that followed, Brooks and I and others made return trips to Petrozavodsk. We learned more about the American Communist movement and about the influence it once had on many in the Upper Midwest. We discovered that Finnish scholars had done a great deal of research on the settlement of Karelia by North Americans, but that not much had been published in the United States. And we found out that Finns were not alone in their fascination with the Soviet experiment. Other North Americans, as well as Europeans, had traveled east in the 1920s and '30s to help Stalin build communism.

The more we learned, the more I felt that a book should be written about the "Karelian fever" that had infected many American and Canadian Finns decades ago.

But who could write such a book? Ideally, it should be done by someone with intimate knowledge of the era, someone with connections to the principal players in the drama, someone who knew English, Finnish and Russian.

I first met Mayme Sevander in 1986 and had visited with her several times after that. But it wasn't until 1989 when Brooks and I were in the Soviet Union for a sister city conference that it struck me that she was in an excellent position to tell the exodus story. Her father was an American radical and a leader in the drive to encourage North American Finns to go to Karelia. She and her family had moved there on one of the last waves of emigration from North America, and she spent the rest of her life as a Soviet citizen. Finally, her language credentials were ideal: Finnish, English, Russian and Swedish.

So Brooks and I worked on Mayme throughout our two-week stay in the Soviet Union. We knew there was a book inside her.

Our efforts paid off. We weren't back in Duluth very long before Brooks received a telex from Mayme stating that she had resigned from her position at the Karelian Pedagogical Institute, would devote the rest of the summer to doing research for the book, and would come to Duluth in the fall to continue her work.

Mayme arrived in November 1989 and—thanks to the generosity of Daniel Pilon, president of the College of St. Scholastica—was given an office near mine.

Laurie Hertzel, a longtime writer and editor for the *Duluth News-Tribune*, joined the project in 1991. Laurie was a member of that first Duluth delegation to visit Petrozavodsk in 1986, and made a return visit five years later.

The result is the volume you are holding in your hands. It is a compelling memoir. More importantly, it's a gesture of reconciliation and peacemaking at the local level.

The events and issues that stand behind Mayme's story were controversial and divisive. Families were split apart in the 1930s over the choice by some to emigrate to Karelia. Hard feelings endured on both sides of the Atlantic throughout subsequent years of persecution and famine under Stalin, the Winter War between the Soviet Union and Finland, the terror of World War II, the McCarthy years of suspicion in the U.S. and the protracted Cold War era that engulfed us all.

Mayme and her family were caught up in that history. Indeed, we all were. Her story contributes to a better understanding of our common past.

> Tom Morgan, associate professor of Russian
> The College of St. Scholastica
> Duluth, Minnesota
> March 1992

The last four years of my life have been devoted to learning the stories of the American Finns who settled in Soviet Karelia. But without the hundreds of letters, photographs, documents and anecdotes that so many of these Finns and their children sent me, this work would have been impossible. I wish there were room to name all of the hundreds of people who contacted me and shared their stories. I thank them all from the bottom of my heart.

I also must thank Dr. Daniel Pilon and Dr. Tom Morgan of the College of St. Scholastica in Duluth. They gave me the means and the opportunity to return to the United States to do this work. Thanks also to Brooks Anderson of the Duluth International Peace Center and his lovely wife, Coral McDonnell, who helped me immeasurably. So many others also opened their homes and hearts to me in Duluth. You understand there is no room to name you all, but you have my undying gratitude.

Mayme Sevander

My heartiest thanks must go to the College of St. Scholastica, for supporting this book in many ways. Thanks also to Pirkko-Liisa O'Rourke at the Finnish Embassy in Washington, D.C., Dr. Reino Kero of the University of Turku, Finland, Dr. Timo Virtanen at the Institute of Migration Studies in Turku, the *Duluth News-Tribune,* and the Global Awareness Fund of the Duluth-Superior Community Foundation.

A number of people took the time to read this manuscript in its various incarnations and give sound advice and suggestions—my brother, David Hertzel, and my good friends, Katy Read, Erik Ninomiya and Pam Miller-Johnson. Ward Melenich made the ultimate sacrifice by allowing me to read huge sections out loud to him. Thanks to you all.

Laurie Hertzel

You Must Remember

My story is one of many.

What happened to me happened to many people, over and over, six thousand times or more, in Pai and Matrosa and Petrozavodsk and Kondopoga and all the other towns and settlements and lumber camps scattered across the Soviet republic of Karelia. You must remember that.

Remember it when I tell you how my father was dragged away from his home in the dark and cold of a bitter November night in 1937. Remember it when I tell you how my brother was thrown into a labor camp, as I was, and how my mother and sister faced death in exile. Remember that these things happened again and again, thousands upon thousands of times, to families of American Finns, like mine, who had gone to Karelia with strong ideals and high hopes. Remember that these things happened more than twenty million times across the Soviet Union during Josef Stalin's dictatorship. If you remember nothing else, remember that.

My father's name was Oscar Corgan. He was born in Nikkala, Sweden, in 1887, the youngest son of a fisherman. Nikkala is a fishing village of wooden houses and birch trees on the Gulf of Bothnia, which separates Finland from Sweden. Though my father lived on the Swedish side of the border, his heritage was Finnish, and he grew up speaking both languages.

Oscar was a thoughtful child and grew to be a serious young man, a deep thinker. You can see it in his face, in pictures of him back then. He had dark hair parted on the side and combed back, and intense eyes under heavy peaked eyebrows. The year he turned twenty, he followed his older brother, Johan, to the United States. They planned to check out America, to see what it offered, to have a few adventures and maybe to make some money. But I think in the back of my father's mind he kept alive the idea that he would someday return home to Sweden. He had no thoughts, back then, of politics. He had no dream, yet, of trying to change the world.

My father was one of thousands of Finns and Swedes who moved to the United States during the late 1800s and early 1900s. Almost 350,000 Finns emigrated during those years, and more than a million Swedes.

In Finland, this was a time of change, an era of economic revolution and depression. Severe famine had hit the country in the 1860s and dragged on for nearly a decade. Year after year, deep, killing frosts froze the fields, and crops withered in the cold. Sons of the destitute farmers abandoned the idea of making a living off the land and began pouring into the cities—Tampere, Turku, Helsinki—looking for work and prosperity. The old Finnish agricultural way of life began to collapse. Many of the young people found jobs in factories, but the work was long and hard and paid very little. Members of this new working class quickly became embittered by what they saw as exploitation by greedy factory owners.

At the turn of the century, Finland was still part of Russia, though it had a great deal of autonomy. But when Oscar was still a boy, Russia began taking a more active role in Finland's internal affairs. In 1901, Russia began conscripting young Finnish men into its army, which contributed to the country's unhappiness. Prompted by economic despair and pushed by Russia's interference, thousands of Finns chose to leave the country, most for America.

The ones who stayed behind faced a hardscrabble life. They were besieged by decades of famine, oppressed by the Russians and looked down upon by the Finnish upper class. Finns were well-educated; even back then, they had to prove they could read and write before they were allowed to marry. And when life turns hard, educated people don't just endure; they look for a better way. For many peasants, tenant farmers, and workers, socialism represented a better way.

By the mid-teens, Finland had become deeply divided. The Red Finns wanted to form a socialist state. The White Finns, the conservative upper class, represented the government. By now, both groups wanted independence from Russia, and both groups wanted control of Finland.

In 1917 and 1918, problems in Russia that had been simmering for years finally came to a head. The czar was overthrown and the country collapsed into chaos. Finland declared its independence from Russia and promptly engaged in its own civil war. In January 1918, the Red Finns attempted a coup, but the White Finns quickly regained control. The civil war was over by May, and the Red Finns began paying the price almost immediately. More than 13,000 of them were killed outright by the White Finns, and 80,000 more were sent to labor camps. In the labor camps, 15,000 people died from disease and malnutrition. The Red Finns began fleeing the country, some to Soviet Russia and others to the United States and Canada.

There were Finns there to meet them in America—emigrants from the first wave, like Oscar Corgan and his brother, who had arrived in the early 1900s. They had settled pockets of Michigan's

Upper Peninsula, Minnesota's Iron Range, the lumber camps of Oregon and the factory towns of Massachusetts. The radicals fleeing Finland joined them there.

North America turned out not to be the land of opportunity the immigrant Finns had envisioned. As one of the last ethnic groups to emigrate from Western Europe, the Finns found that the best farmland and jobs had already been taken. The places that did hire them didn't treat them well; in the American cities, laborers were treated badly and immigrant laborers even worse. It was the age of sweat shops, robber barons, management goons and child labor; it was one of the most exploitative times America has ever known.

But the Finns don't take injustice lying down. Encouraged by *Tyomies* (Working Man) and *Eteenpain* (Forward), the leftist Finnish-language newspapers that were distributed throughout the United States, many Finnish immigrants joined the international union, the Industrial Workers of the World, the American Socialist party, and, a little later, the Communist party. They set up cooperative stores, and they put up community halls, which became centers for radical thought. And they kept up with events at home. They looked with interest at the changes that were going on in Russia, where the working class was rising up in protest.

It was in Hancock, Michigan, that my father, who had come to America with the earlier wave of Finns, first encountered socialism.

Oscar Corgan was twenty years old in 1907, when he first set foot in America. He could speak no English, but he was confident of finding work. He was young and strong, intelligent and hardworking, and wasn't that what was supposed to matter in America, the land of opportunity? What's more, he was educated and could read and write in two languages. Perhaps that's one reason why he went to Hancock: The place was teeming with Finns, and he knew he would feel right at home.

Hancock was a rough-and-tumble town, a cluster of wooden buildings on Michigan's rugged Upper Peninsula. The town was

crowded with saloons and hard-working immigrant miners looking for somewhere to spend their pay.

Oscar found a room in a boardinghouse for Finnish bachelors
and went to work in a copper mine. It was terrible work, grueling
and dangerous. The miners toiled in airless, pitch-black tunnels
deep beneath the earth with only candles affixed to their hard hats
for illumination. Many died underground, killed by explosions or
cave-ins. Some men couldn't tolerate such confinement and quit.
Others stuck it out, hoping to advance into a foreman's job. But
without English-language skills, that was impossible; the otherwise
educated Finns found themselves swinging pickaxes and sweating
in tunnels, while the illiterate—but English-speaking—Welsh,
Irish and Cornish immigrants were given jobs as foremen. It did
no good to complain. There were few unions then, and any
disgruntled worker could easily be replaced. With such a ready
supply of labor, mine owners had no incentive to improve conditions. Management held all the cards.

Was that when my father's radicalism first ignited? Or did it
unfold gradually as he read the only newspapers he could—highly
political Finnish-language papers, such as the socialistic *Tyomies*
and the communistic *Eteenpain?* These newspapers kept readers
apprised of the gains being made by the Bolsheviks in the Soviet
Union, singing the praises of the "workers' paradise" there, where
all men and women were equal and treated with respect, and where
everyone worked hard and got along. The papers also criticized the
corrupt conditions in Finland and the United States, where workers were exploited and Reds were persecuted.

My father wasn't the only Finn to become politicized in those
years. Politics permeated every aspect of life—not just the newspapers, but also the workplace and the community halls, where
Finnish Marxists such as Yrjo Sirola and Santeri Nuorteva tried to
organize the workers into unions. Conditions in the mines and
lumber camps were so terrible that it was easy to see why the

organizers were often successful. Not only were the Finns relegated to the most menial ranks of labor, but they were protected by almost no safety rules or precautions. It became increasingly clear that the lumber barons and mining kings considered workers' lives expendable. Workers who went on strike—as many angry Finns did—were blacklisted from the mines and forced to move on.

My father had been raised to work hard and to be loyal, honest and kind. I can only imagine how these injustices must have affected him, how the union organizers' speeches might have influenced his idealistic mind. All I really know is that he enrolled in night school to study English and started taking classes at a Marxist school in Hancock. And that was the beginning of Oscar Corgan's new life.

I wish I knew how my parents met, who introduced them or at what event they first caught sight of each other. I've been told that it was love at first sight, and that I can well imagine: two handsome, independent young workers who spoke the same language and dreamed the same dreams.

My mother's name was Katri Alalauri and she was from Finland.

She was a beautiful woman, with large eyes and thick, dark hair swept back and coiled over her ears. She was also strong-willed, with an adventuresome streak. Katri was born into utter poverty in the town of Lumijoki, in the Oulu district of Finland. Her parents were farmers, barely scraping a living out of the drought-stricken land, growing just enough to feed their seven children. When my mother was young, she used to help her mother tend the kitchen garden. And as she hoed potatoes and thinned carrots and pulled weeds, she would look up at the sky and dream of a better life.

In 1910, Mother's eldest sister, Maria, married Antti Nissinen and left Finland for Hancock, Michigan. Not long after, Katri followed. She and her older sister, Anna, packed up their few dresses and moved to the United States. They shortened their last name to Lauri and found jobs as maids in a Hancock boarding-house—perhaps the same boardinghouse my father lived in.

That might be where they met. Or perhaps they met at the Finn Hall, the social center of the immigrants' lives. Every town that had Finns had a Finn Hall, and some towns had two. Many immigrant groups put up community halls, but the Finns took it further than any other group. It was at the halls that Finns got together to dance and play music, to talk and listen to lectures. Many of the larger halls had their own choirs, orchestras and amateur brass bands. Sometimes hall-goers staged plays, and my mother, who was very theatrical, often took part. Some Finn Halls held athletic events—races and baseball games and hiking trips.

At the Finn Halls there were no slick management bosses, no loudmouthed foremen, no upper-crust snobs to look down their noses at the Finns. Just Finns and friends of Finns, all speaking Finnish and passing the time over a cup of coffee and a slice of *pulla* (coffee cake).

As time went on, the halls became the centers of radicalism. More and more often, the halls sponsored lectures from people like Nuorteva and Sirola, the Finnish agitators who talked about unions, strikes, socialism and the Bolshevik Revolution. People brought in pictures and, later, films of life in the Soviet Union, or the latest copies of the leftist newspapers.

But the halls weren't without controversy.

Not all Finns were political, and not all Finns approved of the leftist lectures and socialist propaganda. Eventually, there was a split among the immigrants, just as there had been a split among them in their homeland. As the halls became more political, the non-political Finns—mostly the churchgoing, temperate Finns—objected. Eventually, two groups emerged. The Hall Finns, also called the Red Finns or the Bad Finns, were militant socialists, highly political and dedicated to making the world a better place for the working man and woman. The Church Finns, also known as the Temperance Finns or the Good Finns, were religious and nonpolitical and believed that drink—not capitalism—was the ruination of mankind.

My parents were Hall Finns. I think they were probably influenced in their political beliefs by my mother's relatives; Antti Nissinen, my Aunt Maria's husband, was as Red as a Red Finn could be, and a strong believer in the dream of the Soviet Union.

Another influence may have been the tumultuous copper strike in nearby Calumet, Michigan, in 1913. The workers there formed a union and went on strike for better conditions and higher pay—because in those days, of course, immigrants earned less money than Americans. The strike dragged on for months. Scab workers were brought in, and there were scuffles and fights and ugly threats of violence. These events were written about extensively in *Tyomies* and *Eteenpain,* and my parents and other Finnish workers all over the country read the details of the tragedy that took place that December.

On Christmas Eve 1913, the striking copper miners gathered at a community hall—not a Finn Hall, this time, but the upstairs of an old wooden Italian Hall—to celebrate the holiday, as well as their union solidarity. And as the children danced around the Christmas tree and their parents laughed and chatted, suddenly a shout broke through the merriment, a single word that cut through the laughter and caused people to freeze in panic and fear. "Fire!" someone yelled from the bottom of the stairs. "Fire!"

The room erupted into chaos. Parents grabbed their children, sweethearts found each other, and everyone headed for the stairs. They raced down the narrow wooden staircase, only to find the door at the bottom barred from the outside. But those still trapped upstairs kept pushing and feet kept moving. The panic grew worse and the crowd more desperate. The stairway filled with people. Some fell, others kept moving, and children screamed and cried in the chaos.

When it was all over, nearly one hundred people were dead,

stomped and trampled in the panic. More than half of the dead were children—Finnish children.

No one had died of burns or smoke inhalation, for there had been no fire. There had only been panic. And while no one ever found out for sure what had happened, the workers were convinced they knew: Management goons, eager to disrupt the meeting and frighten the striking miners, had shouted the dreaded word "Fire!" and then held the doors of the old wooden hall closed as people tried to escape.

I know my father, and I know my mother, and I know that this kind of violent injustice would have brought anger to my father's spirited, intelligent eyes and caused my mother's lips to press together in white-hot anger. I am sure events like these convinced them that the American dream was no dream at all and that the answer to the problems of class conflict lay in the equality and respect and cooperation promised by socialism.

Big Red, Little Red

I was born in 1923 in the sleepy river town of Brule, Wisconsin, but my earliest memories are of Superior. Superior is a small, flat town in northwestern Wisconsin—not a beautiful city, but a place surrounded by beauty, by nature at its most rugged and wild: the tall Norway pines of the forest, the rocky shore of Lake Superior. Gulls screeched in July and the wind howled in November. It is a town of hard winters and brief, muggy summers. I remember fighting that winter wind as it swept, unchecked, down those flat city streets, a wind so strong you could hardly step into it and cold enough to take your breath away.

We lived in a small, third-floor apartment of the *Tyomies* newspaper building on Tower Avenue. My father was editor and manager of the paper, which was published in Finnish and devoted to the socialist cause. Even back then, my father was my hero. I loved my mother, of course, and her strong, quiet ways, but it was my father I identified with. I used to follow him to work in the mornings, down two flights of stairs to the newspaper office. I was just a little thing, six-years-old, no taller than a tabletop, with perfectly straight white-blonde hair and anxious blue eyes. I loved to sit on the floor amid the clutter of paper and the ringing phone and the smell of ink, drawing pictures on newsprint while my father worked. He'd roll up his shirt sleeves and loosen his tie and become so absorbed in what he was doing that he barely noticed I was there. I felt safe and happy in his company.

It must have been a hectic time for my parents. They were married in Hancock in 1912, and by 1927 they had four children—my brothers Leo and Paul, my little sister, Aino, and me. My family had moved often: from Hancock to Brule, back to Hancock, and then to Superior. My father had quit his job in the mines, worked on the railroad a while, and now was working hard for the socialist cause. He had joined the American Communist party in 1919, the year it was formed, and soon after became a professional party worker, working first as director of the Brule cooperative store and then as manager of *Tyomies*. The Communist party sent him all around the Upper Midwest and relied on him quite heavily as a lecturer. He was a fine public speaker and fluent in three languages, now that he had mastered English.

My father's job as a party worker brought in much less pay—only half as much as he was making on the railroad—but that wasn't important to my parents. We had enough to eat, a warm place to live and clothes on our backs. Our apartment was small, and money was tight, but Mother was a shrewd shopper and smart with a soup bone. We always had enough for a hot supper and a little money left over to donate to the cause.

My parents knew everybody in Superior, it seemed. Our little apartment was always full of people—either my relatives visiting from their farms outside of town, or my parents' socialist friends, or sometimes a stranger in need of a meal and a place to sleep. They would come for dinner and stay late into the night, drinking tea and talking about things I didn't yet understand. I didn't know much about politics, but I did know that we were socialists and proud of it. There were some socialist virtues that had been drilled into me from birth: Help your neighbor, be honest and true, share what you have with those who are less fortunate, and value people and cooperation above material wealth. My parents lived that philosophy, and we were expected to live it, too.

Those were such happy days, when my family was all together. My mother had her hands full with the four of us, and Leo and I, being oldest, had our own chores. My job was to keep the bathroom clean, and every Saturday I'd go to work with a rag and cleanser, though I was barely tall enough to reach the sink. The four of us children shared a bedroom, and my Uncle Peter's daughter, Irene, slept on the couch. She was staying with us while she attended teacher's college in Superior.

Uncle Peter, who had emigrated to America with my father and worked as a laborer in Hancock and Superior, had died several years before I was born. His body was found on a Superior side street one winter's day; he had been shot. The murder was never solved. My parents always spoke of him with affection mixed with exasperation. Peter was a fun-loving, hard-headed man, they said, and his death was made even more tragic by the fact that he left behind two young daughters.

Uncle Peter had never agreed with my father on socialism. The two brothers had been close for years, but when my father took up the cause of socialism, Peter wanted nothing more to do with him. He even changed his last name to Corrigan to keep people from associating him with his brother, Oscar Corgan.

Father never blamed Peter. "We all have to make up our own minds," he would say. And after Peter's death, my parents took in his young daughter, Irene, and gave her a place to stay for as long as she needed it.

In the evenings, my father and I sat quietly and read while Irene studied and Leo practiced the violin; even at this young age he was a brilliant musician, and everyone said he had quite a future ahead of him. My father had a complete English-language collection of the works of Lenin and Marx which he pored over by lamplight at night. I was just beginning to read, but I already had access to quite a few books, and I would sit across the table from my father and page through Leo's volumes of James Fenimore Cooper. We also had a wonderful, big, leatherbound book called *Gems of the World's Best Classics,* which contained bits of everything from Milton and Shakespeare to Tolstoy and Flaubert. That book, my parents told us, would prepare us for our college education some-day. I was too young to read it, but I liked turning its thin pages and looking at its engravings, wondering if I would ever be smart enough to read all those printed words.

As I grew older, if my father caught me reading dime novels or other books he considered trash, he took them away from me and pitched them into the wood stove. He had clear ideas of what was and what wasn't appropriate for children.

Mother was always busy; I never saw her idle. She was always darning socks or baking or cleaning or tending to baby Aino. I admired her sacrifice and hard work, but I knew in my heart that I could never be that way myself. I think the only free time she had to sit and read was long after the four of us were in bed, and I didn't think I could bear that. Even at six, I was beginning to understand the value of books and the joy of reading.

Some evenings my parents headed off to the Finn Hall for a lecture or a concert, leaving Leo in charge. The Finn Hall was just down the block, a big brick building on Tower Avenue, and I remember watching them from the window as they walked up the street, holding hands, sometimes, as they set out for an evening together. My father looked distinguished in his dark coat and tie, and my mother walked beside him, elegant in her long skirts and upswept hair, and happy. After they were gone, I would tag after Leo to the kitchen, where he taught me to make chocolate apples, fudge and custard pie.

Mother spent a lot of time with the Communist Women's Organization, and Father, of course, had *Tyomies* and his lecturing. But every now and then they'd find time for an evening out together. When they returned, they would find a fresh-baked pie on the table waiting for them, a welcome home from Leo and me.

In the winter I took dancing lessons, and summers we sometimes escaped the heat by camping and swimming at Pike Lake in Minnesota. One summer Leo and I spent a week or two at the Young Pioneers Camp in Mesaba Park near Hibbing. I remember the big red flag with the gold hammer and sickle that we flew, and I remember the sky-blue skirt I wore, and the red kerchief that meant I was a Young Pioneer. And I remember the camp songs we sang that said we were proud to be Communists.

The membership card we each were issued laid out what it meant to be a Young Pioneer. Even today, it sounds quite noble: A Young Pioneer fights for food and clothing for children of the unemployed, fights against racial discrimination and for better education for all. I wore my kerchief proudly.

It was after we moved from the *Tyomies* building to a rented house on John Avenue in Superior that I decided to give religion a try. I was quite young still, of course, but old enough to know that my parents wouldn't approve of churchgoing. Like all Communists, my father felt religion was a bourgeois tool used to distract workers from the struggle for their rights.

Our neighbors on John Avenue were the Petersons, a Swedish couple with three children. I used to play with their daughters, Alice and Annette, who were almost my age. When the Petersons discovered we were "godless Socialists," as they called it, they decided to take me in hand. I was curious about religion—I knew that my father had attended church when he was a child, though I'd never been to one—so I agreed to go with them to the Lutheran church not far away. They took me there five or six Sundays in a row before my parents found out. I thought the red brick church quite beautiful inside, though it was difficult for me to sit still through the lengthy service.

When my parents discovered I'd been attending church, I was terrified. My father never yelled at me and never spanked us (though Mother would occasionally give us a swat when she became exasperated), but I knew I'd gone against his beliefs, and I didn't know how he would react.

He didn't get angry, or if he did, he didn't show it. He just spoke to me very seriously. "Mayme," he said. "Communists are atheists. We do not believe in God, and we don't go to church. You cannot grow up between two religions." That was all he said, but it was enough. I could not bear my father's disapproval. I stopped going to church. My father was a man of convictions. There was no discrepancy between his beliefs and his life, and he would allow no discrepancy in ours.

I don't remember when my father first mentioned the Soviet Union, but I do remember that as I grew older I heard the words "Karelia" and "Soviet Union" more and more often. At night I would lie in bed and listen to the voices filtering in from the living room. Leo, Paul and Aino slept nearby, and I could hear their regular, even breathing in the dark. But I tried hard to stay awake, straining my ears to hear what my parents were saying as they sat up late at night with their friends. I felt safe and warm, deep among my blankets, with the light of the living room lamp glowing softly, and the murmur of husky voices.

One of the speakers was Martti Hendrickson, a Communist organizer known throughout the United States. And sometimes I would hear the voice of Vaino Finberg, another Communist whose daughter, Helvi, I knew. I would listen while my father talked passionately about the problems of the working class, the need for trade unions and better working conditions and a fairer distribution of the world's wealth. My father was generally a quiet man at home, but when he started talking about politics and socialism, his voice would grow passionate, and the words would tumble out with urgency and fire. It didn't matter what he was talking about; I felt that I could lie in the dark and listen to him forever.

Sometimes I heard Henry Puro's voice as he and my father

discussed the Bolshevik Revolution and the workers' paradise that lay across the ocean. Puro occasionally visited us from Massachusetts, where he edited the leftist newspaper *Eteenpain*. Most people knew him as John Wiita, the Communist organizer from Canada, but I knew him as a friend. He was a tall, lanky fellow, with the calloused hands of a worker and a strong Finnish accent. He had edited *Tyomies* before my father, but he left for Canada in 1914, when World War I broke out, to avoid being drafted. He changed his name to Puro to keep from being caught and kept that name after he returned to the United States in the 1920s.

One time when I was five or six Puro took me across the bay of Lake Superior to Duluth, Minnesota. He gave me a tour of the Work People's College in the Smithville neighborhood, where he had attended school. It was a wonderful day, just Puro and me in the warm summer sunshine, exploring the green hills of Duluth that were so unlike the plains of Superior. It was thrilling to drive across the long wooden bridge that spanned the bay. We were high above the water, and the gulls soared and shrieked above our heads.

We got home around midnight, and by then the police had already been looking for me for several hours. I had told Puro that it was fine with Mother and Father that he take me, but I had neglected to check with them. I hadn't wanted to take the chance they would say no.

That's the way I was, as a child—not irresponsible, really, but adventuresome and independent. I got my strong-mindedness from my father; we were very much alike.

Our family's happy days in Superior ended abruptly in 1929. That was the year I turned six, and the year my brother died. Leo had always been my mother's favorite—the first-born, the eldest son—just as I was my father's favorite. That autumn he fell ill with edema. The illness moved swiftly. I remember those days as a dark blur of worry and sadness. Our family doctor, Dr. Orchard, called in a specialist from Chicago, but there was nothing he could do. Three days, and Leo was dead. He was eleven years old.

His teacher, Marie Kennedy, brought the entire sixth-grade class to the funeral, where Leo lay in his little white coffin. It was a harsh autumn day with a raw wind, and I remember Leo's violin teacher, Mr. Fisher, crying nearly as hard as my parents at Greenwood Cemetery outside of town. When we got home, my mother took down Leo's violin from its place on top of the bookcase and handed it to me. "You must learn to play now, Mayme," she said, a catch in her voice. "It's up to you to pick up where Leo left off." She turned in tears and ran into her bedroom. And I was left standing in the living room, a six-year-old child holding a violin and missing her brother with all her heart.

My mother was not the same after that. She grew quieter and sadder, and she said there was no way she could continue to live in Superior. My father quit *Tyomies*, and we moved to a small frame house in Virginia, a town on Minnesota's Iron Range, where he became director of the cooperative store.

My family's connection with *Tyomies* continued, however, for my little brother, Paul, began selling the newspaper on the street corners. Paul used to follow our father around the house in the mornings when Father was getting ready for work, trying to walk just like him. He'd turn up his collar and swing his arms and strut past me like a miniature grownup. He told Father that by selling the newspapers, he was helping the party cause.

I reluctantly took up the violin, but what had been a graceful, lovely instrument in my brother's hands became a clumsy, screeching thing in mine. I don't know what pained my mother more—to hear me practice or to think I was shirking my lessons. I tried, I really did, but my hands were small, and my heart wasn't in it. It was Leo's violin, not mine, and it always would be.

After we moved to Virginia, Father was gone more often. The party sent him on more lecture trips across the Upper Midwest, and when I grew a little older, I started going with him.

I felt proud, climbing into his old black Ford to head for the

Finn Hall in Duluth or Hibbing or Calumet, Michigan. I waved goodbye to Mother, who was holding Aino, and to Paul, who I liked to think was vastly jealous, and then climbed in next to my father. The trips were long, and I often fell asleep in the car, but I think my father was glad to have the companionship.

At the time, I didn't really understand what Father was lecturing about, but the trips were exciting anyway. The Finn Halls were always lit up, the smell of hot coffee wafted out into the night, and the Finns showed up from miles around to hear Father speak. Outside there were cars and horse carts waiting, and inside there was someone to lead my father to the platform and introduce him to the crowd.

A meeting would typically last for hours. I would usually go into the children's room, play with the other kids and have a snack.

But sometimes I listened. And when I did, I heard Father talking about Karelia, the part of the Soviet Union that bordered Finland. Karelia was looking for workers—loggers and fishermen, primarily—and Father's job was to let Finnish workers know that they were more than welcome in the Soviet Union.

Karelia needs you, Father always told the crowds in the overflowing Finn Halls. It needs strong workers who know how to chop trees and dig ore and build houses and grow food. Isn't that what we Finns have been doing in the United States for the past thirty years? And wouldn't it be wonderful to do that same work in a country that needs you, a country where there is no ruling class, no rich industrialists or kings or czars to tell you what to do? Just workers toiling together for the common good.

Though most of the republics of the Soviet Union were looking for workers in those days, my father's talks focused on Karelia because immigration to this area was part of a plan being promoted by Finnish Communist leaders in the Soviet Union. Karelia was a huge, lush wilderness, dotted with lakes and rich with pine and birch. But the five-year plan the government had established set ambitious goals for timber production. It would clearly be impossible to meet those goals with the people and equipment the region now had. Karelia was sparsely populated, settled mostly by ethnic Russian and Karelian peasants. They were primarily unskilled laborers and had almost no machinery or equipment. The old logging methods they followed were slow and inefficient; working in crews of two, lumberjacks felled only two or three trees a day between them. And there were no good roads and no trucks or sleds large enough to transport the trees they did take down.

The two men who headed the Karelian government at this time—Edvard Gylling and Kustaa Rovio—were Finnish Communists, and the idea to recruit American and Canadian Finns may well have come from them. In many ways, the plan made great sense to both American Finns and to the Soviets. Finns had long been attracted to Karelia, which was where the Finnish epic poem, the *Kalevala,* originated. The ethnic Karelians spoke a language similar to Finnish, so communication would be easy. Finns were known to be hard workers—excellent fishermen and loggers, which is exactly what Karelia needed. Many of the American and Canadian Finns could afford to buy their own saws, tractors and logging equipment to bring with them. And, of course, many Finns were radicals—strong believers in socialism, who saw the Soviet Union as the place where their Utopian dreams could come true. The whole program happened to coincide with the Great Depression, as well, which made the chance to emigrate from America even more attractive.

So the recruiting agency Karelian Technical Aid was born, with offices in New York and Toronto. The agency worked with the Immigration Department in the Karelian capital of Petrozavodsk. Between 1930 and 1934, recruiters like my father visited Finn Halls across the United States and Canada, letting Finns know how much their help was needed by their brothers in Karelia. Karelia wasn't just looking for loggers and fishermen, though those were of primary importance; Rovio and Gylling were hoping to attract skilled workers of all kinds: machinists, metalworkers, mechanics, carpenters, plumbers. There would be plenty of work for all in Petrozavodsk and the surrounding communities.

My father was an excellent speaker, inspiring but temperate. He never made promises that couldn't be kept, and he warned people that life in the Soviet Union would be primitive. The Soviet Union is a brand new country, he told them, and Karelia is an unsettled area. It'll be like being pioneers all over again—log cabins, no electricity, a struggle to make ends meet, and work, lots of bone-tiring hard work, from morning till night. He told them that Soviet Karelia is bitter cold in the winter—as cold and dark as Finland or Minnesota—and that food and clothing would be in short supply until things got off the ground.

The people listened eagerly. Some of them were homesick for Finland and were attracted by the idea of moving to Karelia, close to their homeland. Many of them were tired of American capitalism and the way immigrants were treated as second-class citizens. And many of them were fervent revolutionaries, strong supporters of the Bolshevik cause and excited at the prospect of creating a new land where workers would rule, where there would be no unemployment or exploitation and where everyone would be comrades.

They always kept my father late, drinking pots of coffee and asking him questions about Karelia, how to get there and what it was like. He told them about Karelian Technical Aid and how it would help them arrange passage, shop for supplies and take care of the details of emigration.

And then my father and I would climb back into the car and I would curl up in the back seat and doze as we bumped home again along rutted, starlit roads, or traveled to the home of a Finnish farmer who had agreed to put us up for the night.

In many ways, my parents were wanderers in America, moving from town to town, looking for a place where they could settle down and do the most good. We didn't stay in Virginia long. The cooperative store was a strong socialist venture, but I don't think it took full advantage of my father's talents. He was more ambitious than that, but his ambitions weren't selfish; they were ambitions for the cause. He wanted to make a difference across the country, not just in one small Minnesota town.

So we moved back to Superior and *Tyomies*. My father was on the road now more than ever, including a trip to the Soviet Union itself, to organize and lecture. He went abroad again in 1932, as a delegate to the Industrial Workers of the World trade union congress in Vienna, Austria, and he visited Moscow a second time.

We began attending Communist rallies in Duluth and Superior, where my father was often a speaker. Occasionally I would speak, too, reciting poetry. At one Superior rally, my father gave a speech, and I stood at his side and recited a poem about Lenin:

> Lenin! Who is that guy?
> He's not big,
> Neither is he high.
> He has two hands
> And a pair of eyes.
> He's just as human
> As you and I

A reporter from Superior's daily paper, the *Evening Telegram,* was there, and the next day my father read aloud his account. The clipping has long since been lost, but I remember that it said something like, "The main address was given by the Big Red, Oscar Corgan, and the secondary address was given by the Little Red, Mayme Corgan." I was pleased. We made such a team, my Big Red father and me.

My father was getting more and more interested in the Karelian project, and each week *Tyomies* and *Eteenpain* were filled with descriptions of developments in Karelia, what goals were being met and how satisfied the workers were to be doing their share.

The emigration movement grew rapidly. By 1932, thousands of Canadian and American Finns had already responded to the call from the Soviet Union. Each family paid a $400 fee to Karelian Technical Aid, packed its belongings and set sail on one of the ships in the Swedish-American line. There were always hundreds of socialists at dockside, waving goodbye and wishing them well. In the holds of the ships were saws, tractors, farming and logging equipment, fishing nets, automobiles and printing presses.

The Finnish newspapers devoted huge ads to the departing groups, printing the names of the emigrants alongside messages of hope and farewell.

At picnics and meetings where Finns gathered to say goodbye to their departing comrades, people sang inspirational songs, like this one, written in Finnish by a now-forgotten person of the time:

> Far away to Asian expanses
> Our comrades are leaving again,
> Knowing so well they stand no chances
> Of winning without taking pains.
>
> Work will begin: axes will fly
> The woods with sounds will ring;
> Hammer-hit anvils will set up a cry
> Furnaces and mines will sing.
> There'll be a contest of sounds
> To proclaim: A republic is found!
>
> Many an obstacle you may not know
> This faraway journey will bring.
> But once overcome, the day will glow
> With created light and workers will sing!

It was a festive, exciting time, a time of hope, and my father was proud to be part of it.

It is hard to say exactly how many American and Canadian Finns moved to the Soviet Union during this time. Most scholars have put the number at about six thousand. Many—perhaps as many as half—of the emigrés returned to the United States within the first two years, disillusioned by the harsh conditions they encountered in Karelia. And, of course, this "Karelian Fever" didn't strike all American Finns. The Church Finns disapproved strongly of the movement to Karelia, to the "godless country" of the Soviet Union. Families split during these years, as the Hall Finns set sail for the new world and the Church Finns stayed behind. In some families, brother turned against brother when one made the decision to go and one to stay. Families were fragmented when parents brought their younger children with them to the Soviet Union but allowed their older children to stay in America to finish school, marry or work.

Though my father was busy and happy during this time, living in Superior again was very hard on my poor mother; it brought back painful memories of Leo and his untimely death. Father's frequent absences must have made coping even more difficult. In 1932, when Kalle Aronen, head of Karelian Technical Aid in New York, emigrated to the Soviet Union with his wife, Hilma, my father was offered his job. Father accepted, and our life in the Midwest was over.

One of the last memories I have of living in Superior was a rally across the bay in Duluth. Hundreds of American Communists gathered on the steps of the Federal Building in Duluth's Civic Center to commemorate the International May Day. I stood at the foot of the statue of Patriotism and waved the red Communist flag with pride as someone snapped my picture.

A few months later, we packed our things, carefully wrapping Leo's violin and our precious framed photograph of him in soft blankets for the journey, and headed for New York City.

The Little Communist

I couldn't believe my luck.

It had been a long, rough journey to New York by car over bumpy two-lane roads, but out of all the things we had brought along, out of all the dishes and photographs and clocks and precious mementos, only one thing had been damaged. We discovered it when my mother unrolled a blanket that contained Leo's things. Out fell Leo's violin. It was broken into two pieces, its neck cracked.

I was secretly delighted, though of course I didn't tell my mother that. After three tortured years of violin lessons, I was finally able to play simple tunes, but all of the instrument's tone and sweetness seemed to have died with Leo. I loved music, but I knew I had no business trying to produce it myself.

"Well, that's that," my mother said with a sigh, laying the ruined violin in a drawer. "Don't worry, Mayme. We'll get it fixed one of these days."

"It's all right," I said, crossing my fingers for luck.

There was so much to do in New York it wasn't surprising that the violin was never mended.

Our first two nights, we stayed with friends, Vaino and Emma Rimpinen, in their Brooklyn cooperative house, "Moscova." Quite a few Finns had started cooperative houses on the East Coast, and they often named them in tribute to the Soviet Union. The Rimpinens were a kind couple, but they had no children and were accustomed to quiet ways. I think my parents were afraid that our large family was quite an imposition. In any case, we didn't stay with them long, but took one of the first apartments we could find—a huge, furnished, eight-room affair not far away. It was quite expensive, and we ended up moving again shortly after, to a more affordable three-room apartment in the Bronx.

My father sold the car and took the subway each morning to the Karelian Technical Aid office in Harlem. He worked such long hours that we seldom saw him. After the first winter we decided that if we ever wanted to spend time with him again, we would have to join him in Harlem, and so we did. We found a nice, roomy apartment on the third floor of a building on 128th Street, just four blocks from the Finn Hall and within walking distance of his workplace.

My father's office at Karelian Technical Aid was a tiny place in the basement of a tenement building on 126th Street. It had a cluttered desk, a typewriter and a battered file cabinet, with a small storeroom in the back.

Just as in the old days at *Tyomies,* I liked hanging around there and stopped by nearly every day after school. Finally my father told me, "Mayme, if you're going to be here taking up space anyway, I might as well put you to work." He told me to sit down at the typewriter. "You could be a big help to me if you'd just learn how to type," he said. "I could really use a secretary."

After that I helped my father every afternoon. I was only nine, but I learned to type, and I began taking care of most of his correspondence, as well as the filing and record keeping. Every day, people came by—American Finns moving to the Soviet Union, or Communist party workers who had business with my father. The

Finns seemed sure of their decision to emigrate but worried about the details, and my father took them all under his wing. "It's not difficult," he told them, "once you get organized. You just have to take it one step at a time." He was so calm and reassuring that they relaxed and placed their confidence in him. He helped them with their applications and paperwork, booked passage for them on the ships, and took them shopping for the supplies and tools they would need.

Sometimes my father and I went to the dock to see the groups off as they set sail for Europe. I was always struck with a twinge of envy: It was festive and cheerful, huge crowds of people hugging each other as they said goodbye. Sometimes a band would play the "Internationale," and everywhere, red handkerchiefs waving in promise and farewell.

My tenth birthday came and went, and I began feeling more at home in New York. The city was quite a change from the Upper Midwest. At first I missed the green of the Iron Range and the quiet pace of Superior. I missed Lake Superior, with its gulls and the mysterious fog that sometimes rolled in and enshrouded the town. I wasn't used to so much concrete, so many cars, so much dirt and litter. It was 1933, the height of the Depression, and I saw despair on the faces of many New Yorkers. Stores were closed, buildings were shuttered, people in dirty clothes and cardboard shoes shuffled past our apartment.

The effects of the Depression were much more evident to us in New York than they had been in Superior, and my parents talked about it nearly every night. One of the problems with capitalism, my father would say again and again, is that there's always someone on the bottom of the heap. And that someone is always the worker. "Look at those people," he'd say whenever a shiny big car drove past. "They're not hurting. They've got fancy clothes and polished shoes and drivers and money to burn. How can this be fair? Why is this allowed? People are starving all around them!"

My mother would shake her head. "They should share what they have," she said. "There's enough to go around, if they'd just redistribute what they have."

I had a friend in the Bronx, a girl named Hortense who lived in a huge, twelve-room apartment in a building with a doorman and a fancy elevator. I don't know what her father did for a living, but it was clear that her parents were rich, and I think they were amused by our friendship. "Here comes Mayme, the little Communist," they would tease whenever I came up to play. And in my fervor, I would remember my parents' words and try to convert them to the socialist cause.

My life in Harlem was divided between school, home and the Finn Hall. My mother still couldn't understand the English language, but the Vuorelas, a friendly Finnish couple, lived just upstairs from us, and the hall was just a few blocks away, so she had plenty of friends. The New York Finn Hall was the grandest I'd ever seen, paid for entirely by donations and built of brick. It was four stories high, with a swimming pool, a sauna, a library, an auditorium, billiard tables and a cafeteria. We ate dinner at the cafeteria most Sunday evenings, to give my mother a break from cooking. And after dinner, Paul and I used to sneak up the stairs to the top floor, where there was a dance hall with a glass ceiling. We were too young to take part ourselves, but we loved to spy on the dancers. We'd sit on the stairs and watch them whirl and turn, with the stars shining down upon them through the roof, and we'd tap our toes in time to the music until our mother found us and sent us back downstairs again.

My best friends in New York were Georgia Washington, Stella Baker and Doris Sutinen. I knew Doris from the Finn Hall—she was taller than I was, with long, curly hair and a ready laugh. We used to go to the movies together, and we were both members of Vesa, the hall's athletic club.

Stella and Georgia were classmates of mine at the school in Harlem. I was the only white girl in my class, and Paul was the only white boy in his. As Communists, we didn't believe in segregation or discrimination, and since the black school was nearer to our apartment than the white school, we went to the black school.

Stella and Georgia and I used to play jacks, stick ball and hopscotch together on weekends. It never occurred to me to feel out of place, even though I was just about the only white girl they knew. The only time the difference between us was apparent was at a party one evening, and even then it wasn't the difference in color that bothered me, but rather the difference in economics.

It was a wonderful party at Stella's apartment, with great things to eat and games to play and lots of other girls to talk to. But one of the first things I noticed when I walked in the door was how beautiful their dresses were. They had actual party dresses, but I was just wearing my best dress from school—it was all I had. Stella and her friends were wearing white organdy dresses with gathered bodices entwined with ribbons and lace, and big white bows in their dark curls. My dress was very simple—plaid, with a round lace collar—and though I had liked it fine when my mother had first made it for me, I suddenly felt homely and plain next to the other girls.

It nearly ruined the party for me. When Stella and Georgia and the other girls took their turn at pinning the tail on the donkey, all I could see were full skirts and swirls of lace. As the afternoon wore on, my dress felt plainer and plainer until I was sure the other girls were all laughing at me—or, even worse, pitying me.

I came home from the party with a long face. My father noticed, and he sat me down on the couch and asked what was wrong. I squirmed a little, because I didn't want to sound like I was complaining, but the words came out as a complaint anyway. "Everyone at the party was better dressed than I was," I said, scuffing my foot on the floor and not looking at him. "Their dresses were so pretty, and mine is just the same old thing from school."

There was such a long silence that I finally looked up, and I was struck by how serious my father looked. His dark eyes, always intense, seemed to be boring right through me. He finally spoke. "How many pairs of shoes do you have, Mayme?" I was surprised by the question. "Two," I said.

He nodded. "And do you have a winter coat to keep you warm?"

"Yes," I said. I didn't really understand what this had to do with organdy party dresses.

He nodded again. "And was the dress you wore to the party clean? Did it fit? Did it have any rips or tears in it?"

"No, it fit," I said. "It's not ripped. But it's ugly and plain. Theirs had ribbons."

My father was silent for awhile again. And then he spoke. "You know, Mayme, there are lots of children going hungry all over the world," he said, and his voice was very serious. "Children without enough to eat, children who don't get a hot bowl of cereal in the morning and a good meal at night, like you do. There are lots of children who don't have any shoes, let alone two pairs, and who don't have any coat at all. With so many children in the world who are doing without, how can you ask for more than you already have? You have so much more than they do."

By now, I was starting to feel ashamed of myself, but my father wasn't done. "That dress you wore to the party isn't fancy," he said. "But it's clean and new. And it's pretty. It looks pretty on you." He pinched my cheek softly. "And you look especially pretty when you smile."

I couldn't help smiling at that. But I also felt ashamed for complaining. "I do like my dress," I told my father, snuggling closer to him on the couch. "I don't think it's ugly." And as I spoke, I realized that it was true. I was proud not to have dozens of dresses, because my family believed in sharing what we had with those who had little, instead of spending every dime on ourselves. In my heart of hearts, I still hoped for an organdy dress, but I no longer felt ashamed of the clothes I had.

We stayed in New York for two years. My parents were never ones to discuss problems or decisions with their children. They believed that adults should govern the family and that children should be good and obedient. But gradually I came to realize that, once again, we were beginning to make preparations for another big move. I just wasn't sure exactly where it was we were moving.

By the beginning of 1934, it was clear that Karelian Technical Aid had served its purpose and was preparing to shut down. There was less work for me to do in the afternoons now, fewer letters to type, and fewer people stopping by to see my father. The huge groups of two hundred and three hundred emigrants had dwindled to groups of fewer than one hundred, and groups were leaving less often than before. Many of our friends, including the Rimpinens and Doris Sutinen and her family, had already emigrated. My father said that in Karelia the need for new workers had dwindled, and Petrozavodsk was having trouble keeping up with housing and supplies for the thousands who had already arrived.

Around this time the Communist party offered my father a job in California. I overheard my parents discussing the offer one evening, and I began to wonder what it would be like to live in a place where oranges and grapefruits grew in my back yard. As winter dragged on and the white snow turned dingy and gray, balmy California seemed more and more attractive.

One blustery March evening a young couple came to our apartment for dinner. They were Finns, activists for the Young Communist League, and they had almost no money. They had been on the road for some time and were ready to settle down in New York, but they had nowhere to live and no money for rent. My father poured them each a cup of tea. "Do you like this place?" he asked them.

The pair looked surprised. They glanced around at our homey apartment with its comfortable, shabby furniture and the heavy drapes that kept out the winter chill. "Well, yes," they said. "But you don't exactly have extra room. We don't want to impose on you."

"Not at all," my father said. "We're leaving. We're sailing for Soviet Karelia on April 4. The rent here is paid through the end of April. You can stay here, if you like. We'll be leaving behind all of the furniture except the big bed, so you don't even have to worry about furnishing it."

The couple was astounded. They had never heard of such generosity, and they tried to stammer out their thanks. My father waved it away. "You'll be doing us a favor," he said, "by taking all this stuff off our hands. We can't take it with us, and now we won't have to worry about selling it off. We can help each other this way."

I didn't say anything—we were still at the dinner table, where children were to be seen but not heard—but I listened for all I was worth. My eyes grow wide with excitement. Karelia! We were actually moving to the Soviet Union! Over the years I had attended so many Pioneer camps, so many Communist rallies, and always, the goals of the Soviet Union and its first leader, V.I. Lenin, had been held out as almost unattainable. And now we were going—we would live these ideals ourselves. I was sure I couldn't wait until April 4.

A few days later, we went out and had our passport picture taken—one of the first family photos we had ever had. My mother tied my straight blonde hair up in rags the night before, and the next morning when she combed it my hair stood out from my head in shoulder-length waves. Aino got her Dutch bob trimmed for the picture, and Paul was told to put on a tie.

The photographer posed us, telling Paul and me to stand in the back and putting Aino up front. And in the middle he placed my parents—my mother, with her big brown eyes staring straight out at the camera; and my father, his face severe under those bristling eyebrows of his. It was a dramatic family portrait, and the last one ever taken of us all.

On our last night in New York, our friends threw the biggest party I had ever seen. The Finn Hall was all lit up, and the tables in the auditorium were spread with white cloths and covered with pots of coffee, platters of cookies, and little bowls of candy. Paul and I had a contest to see who could eat more cookies, but little Aino took a fancy to the tiny green mints and crammed them into her mouth until her lips turned green. More than four hundred people packed into the hall to say goodbye to my father, and we listened to speech after speech until we were yawning so hard we thought our faces would split.

My last observation before I fell asleep on a chair in the corner was of one of my father's friends, standing next to my father on the stage. "Let's hear it for Oscar Corgan!" the man was shouting, and everyone in the room let out a cheer.

Pioneers Again

I stood on the deck, sea spray in my face, the pitch and roll of the waves under my feet, and I was perfectly happy. We had left New York late on the afternoon of April 4, 1934, sailing away from a beautiful sunset. Hundreds of people had come down to the dock to see us off, and we waved our red handkerchiefs at them until they were just dots in the distance. The pinks and yellows and oranges spread out behind us across the western sky and reflected on the calm ocean. It seemed like a good omen and a wonderful farewell, but the weather changed overnight. A strong wind came up, the sky grew dark and gray, and I awoke to a tremendous rain.

For eight days we crossed the ocean, and for eight days it stormed. Mother, Paul and Aino lay in their bunks and moaned from seasickness. Father and I donned our waterproof coats and wandered the pitching, slippery decks, watching the sailors work, looking out at the gray, choppy ocean, tasting its salty spray. I was cheerful and happy, thinking about the adventure that lay ahead, but my father was quiet and thoughtful.

I had been content in New York, but I was excited to travel. I had heard so much about the Soviet Union and how my old friends from Wisconsin, Minnesota and New York were now living a happy life there, working hard and building a new society. For two years I had watched people I knew leave—friends of my parents, who had spent nights at our apartment in Superior while waiting to catch a ride to New York, or children I had played with at the Young Pioneers Camp. It had been two years already since Ruth Niskanen had left; she was from Palo, Minnesota, and I remember that her family stayed with us in Superior one cold January, waiting to leave for New York. While our parents talked in the front room, Ruth and I made fudge and talked about what she thought Karelia would be like. And my friend Irma Tenhunen was gone, too. Her father had been the first to head Karelian Technical Aid, and they'd been gone since 1931. And Helvi Finberg, whose family stayed with us on their way from Astoria, Oregon. Helvi was six years older than me, and I always secretly admired her clothes and hairstyles. And Hilda Martin from Cloquet, Minnesota; and Roy Siikki from Zim, Minnesota. One by one, people I had served tea to in my parents' living room or had played with at summer camp or had attended concerts with at the hall had left the country. It seemed like everyone I knew was gone.

For two years, I had been reading in *Tyomies* the long lists of names of families that had emigrated. There were thousands of them. I had read some of the letters they sent back to the newspaper, all about the struggles and hardships they were overcoming there, and about how wonderful it felt to be building a new society. Some of the groups left farewell messages behind in *Tyomies,* like this one I tore out and saved from the Oct. 3, 1931, issue:

> We the undersigned, leaving behind this country of capitalistic exploitation, are headed for the Soviet Union, where the working class is in power and where it is building a socialistic society. We appeal to you, comrades, who are staying behind, to rally round communist slogans, to work efficiently to overthrow capitalism and create the foundation of a Republic of Labor.

It all sounded inspiring to me. And now it was our turn. I was still a child, of course, only eleven years old, and I didn't really understand the concepts of freedom and socialism and equality. But I knew my father believed in them, and I knew my mother did, and I knew that when I was old enough, I would, too.

On the ninth day we landed in Göteborg, a seaport on the western shore of Sweden. My mother, brother and sister emerged from the cabin, pale and shaky but otherwise fine. All around us was the hustle and bustle of shipbuilding and commerce, people hurrying past us, the smell of new wood and sawdust and the salty tang of ocean in the air. We rounded up our trunks and luggage and the printing press that Father had bought in New York as his contribution to the new Petrozavodsk society, and we found a room to stay in until we could take the train to Stockholm.

Sweden, even in the chilly dampness of early spring, was beautiful, especially after the everlasting grayness of New York. Here, everything was budding and green. The clouds broke up, and the weather cleared, and the ocean lay before us, sparkling blue and white. At breakfast, I couldn't drink enough of the good Swedish milk; it was so rich and tasty. Everything seemed clean and fresh and new. I was excited and wanted to explore this country where my father had been born.

But oddly enough, my father didn't want us to explore.

After several days in Göteborg, we took the train to Stockholm and stayed there for a week at the Ambassador Hotel, waiting for a ship that would take us across the Baltic Sea and the Gulf of Finland to Leningrad. Nearly every day, the telephone in our hotel room jangled, and the caller turned out to be one or another of Father's relatives up north, urging us to come and visit his old home in Nikkala. Father's mother had died while he was in America, but his father was still living there, as were his sisters, Anna and Marianna. His brother, Johan—the one he used to compete with in school, the one he had followed to America—had returned to Sweden several years ago and was living nearby, carrying on the family fishing trade. All of them called us, again and again, telling us how much they would love to see us and reminding us that the trip was just a few hours' journey by train.

Paul and I were both eager to go. We thought Sweden was great, but we were getting bored hanging around the hotel waiting for a ship that seemed like it would never arrive. "Can't we go visit?" we asked, as often as we dared. We'd been taught not to whine, but this was almost irresistible. We used every wheedle we could think of: "We've never seen our grandpa! We want to see our cousins! We want to go fishing!"

I think my mother wanted to visit, too, though she wouldn't say; she would never cross Father on something as important as this. His word was law, and in this case, the word was no. But her family home lay just a few hundred kilometers away, across the gulf in Finland, and it must have been tantalizing to her to be so close to her family and yet unable to see them. She hushed us, though, and told us to enjoy our time in Stockholm. We would be leaving soon enough, she told us, and we could always come back and visit our grandpa later.

Looking back, I think I understand my Father's dilemma. I think he knew by now that the Soviet Union wasn't going to be the place he had worked so hard to create. He had been there twice already, and he had talked with groups of American Finns who had emigrated and then changed their minds and returned to America. My father was idealistic, but he was also clear-eyed. I think he knew there would be problems and that he was bringing his family to a place of uncertainty and struggle, perhaps even danger.

But what else could he do? He had encouraged so many hundreds of families to go to Karelia, told them of life in the Soviet Union, helped them get passage on board the ships, helped them find their way from the copper mines of Calumet and the iron mines of Tower-Soudan and the farms and shops of Embarrass and Palo and Hibbing and Brule and Superior all the way to New York and then on across the ocean. He had to join them. For better or worse, he had to follow his ideals. To do less would have been hypocritical, and my father was no hypocrite.

But to visit his beloved family home in Nikkala—oh, how strong would my father have to be to leave his family again, to return to his father's house and then leave it for an uncertain life in a foreign country. Every human being has a weakness, and I think my father's weakness was his family. I'm sure he was afraid that if we went to his home, his aging father and his brother and sisters would put pressure on him to stay—or at least to leave us children there. And I think he was afraid that he would end up giving in.

So he took a firm stand. We could not visit Nikkala. He never explained why. We were waiting for the boat. That was all.

We hadn't been at the hotel more than a couple of days when two men showed up to visit my father. I peered out at them from behind the door: tall men, distinguished-looking, with dark hair and dark mustaches. They were wearing the whitest shirts I'd ever seen, and tall hats and expensive coats and shiny black shoes. My father was not a nervous person, but he was nervous around these men. He invited them in and they sat and talked for the longest time in the fragile chairs of the hotel parlor. Eavesdropping did me no good; these men spoke to my father in Swedish, which none of us children understood. That night at supper, my mother asked him who they were.

"Oh, they're just trying to get us to stay here in Sweden," he said, and he wouldn't talk about it further. The men came again, and again, and each time my father grew tense and nervous, but each time he firmly told them no, we were going on.

One afternoon a group of Americans arrived at our hotel. There were lots of them—at least a hundred—and they were from

Petrozavodsk, the Karelian capital, where we were headed. They were an unhappy group, bitter and disillusioned with the Soviet Union, and they were going back to America. My father met with the group and tried to talk to them.

Suddenly one of the men burst out at him in anger. "Some paradise! Some utopia! Everything you told us was a pack of lies! There's no paradise there! Do you know what it's like? Do you have any idea what it's really like there?"

Before my father could respond, one of the man's companions interrupted. "Stop it," he said, laying a hand on his friend's shoulder. "He didn't lie to us. If we had listened to the words of Oscar Corgan, we would never have gone. He told us it wouldn't be easy. Don't you remember when he said it would be just like being pioneers again? He promised no paradise. We just didn't listen."

I listened to the yelling, and I shivered inside. What lay ahead of us? What could be so terrible as to make them turn around and go home again? Wasn't a country of workers worth sacrificing and working hard for? I had always believed that it was, but these people looked desperately unhappy. And I was all the more curious to get to the Soviet Union and see for myself.

After waiting a week, we got word that we could catch a ride the next day on the Soviet icebreaker *Spartak*. It was a rather unorthodox way of traveling, but it would get us and our belongings to Leningrad. The next morning, the two mysterious men showed up at our hotel one last time. They took us to the pier in their big, shiny car. And they were still talking earnestly to my father, right up to the last minute. My father was less nervous now, and seemed more resolved. Now that the moment of truth had come, he was assured and calm.

As we boarded the icebreaker, one of the men stopped me. "Take this," he said in English, handing me a huge paper bundle. He had similar bundles for Paul and Aino. "And remember, you won't have anything of this kind when you get over there." He patted me on the head and drove off.

On board the boat, we opened our bundles and found all kinds of wonderful things to eat—smoked chicken; chocolates; hard candy; huge, bright oranges; and the yellowest, firmest bananas. I never found out who those men were. Perhaps they were father's cousins, trying to persuade him to stay in Sweden. Perhaps they were party members, trying to tell him that he would be more useful as an organizer outside of the USSR. I don't know. But they were right about one thing: In Karelia, there were no oranges or bananas. In Karelia, there was no fresh fruit at all.

Filled With Hope

Leningrad, when we arrived, was gray and dusty and crowded. The wind was cold and blew grit into our eyes. Trolley buses, packed with passengers, rattled past us down the main street, Nevsky Prospekt, their cables spitting sparks above our heads. I couldn't read the street signs—the alphabet looked backwards to me—or understand the conversations I overheard in the train station. It all seemed exotic and foreign, but it was wearying as well. I was anxious to get to our new home.

After two days in a Leningrad hotel, where Mother rested and Father attended to business, we boarded the overnight train for Petrozavodsk. It was actually much longer than an overnight trip; the eighteen hours we spent on that train felt like an eternity, especially for my brother and me, who were accustomed to running about and playing. It was tedious, sitting still on those hard wooden benches hour after hour as the train jolted and shook and the people around us dozed or took bites from hunks of sausage and cheese they had stashed in their bags.

The train traveled on north, stopping to pick up passengers in villages along the way and sometimes stopping for no reason at all.

Paul and I tried to sleep—we wrapped ourselves in blankets and stretched out on the benches—but every so often the train shivered and shook and jolted us awake again, piercing our dreams with its long, mournful whistle. My mother held Aino and tried to keep her from crying. I know Mother was very tired. My father looked out the grimy train window, his eyes dark and stern under his heavy black eyebrows, and he didn't speak.

I got up and stood beside my father to look out at the Russian countryside. It was evening, and the light outside was dim, but it was still bright enough to see. I rubbed a clean spot on the window with my index finger and pressed my nose to the glass. Everything was lovely and rugged. It was easy to pretend that I was the first person ever to have traveled there. The land looked untouched. I'd never seen pine trees so tall, or forests so dense. We clattered across a rickety wooden bridge, and I looked down and saw a river roaring past far below, wild with spring runoff. We passed little communal farms carved out of the forest, and I saw women with rubber boots and kerchiefs digging the ground, getting ready for planting.

On April 30, 1934, we arrived in Petrozavodsk, grimy and wrinkled and stiff from the long train ride. Kalle Aronen, my father's predecessor at Karelian Technical Aid, met us at the station and brought us home with him.

All the way to his house, I looked around me, wide-eyed, at the city that was to be my new home. Petrozavodsk was a city of about twenty thousand people. It looked somehow medieval. The main streets were cobblestone, but the rest of the roads were dirt, with car tracks and the clear prints of horses' hooves in the dust. There were no sidewalks. Most of the houses were small, unpainted log homes with shingled roofs and dirty windows. Smoke from a thousand chimneys rose straight up into the clear evening sky. It didn't look like New York, and it didn't look like Sweden, but I was excited to be there at last.

The Aronens lived in a cooperative house—two rooms with a kitchen, and a shared privy out back. Kalle Aronen's wife, Hilma, fed us a supper of boiled potatoes and sour brown bread—not very American, but hot and filling. I was so hungry I ate it all and then fell asleep almost immediately. In the morning, I awoke to find my mother smiling at me and telling me to get dressed. "Mayme, it's May Day!" she cried.

The sun shone down warmly and the grass had a green haze of new growth. My friend from New York, Doris Sutinen, came over, and we went off together to attend the festivities. All the children of the American Finns were there, dressed in white, and they sang and danced. Doris's long curls bounced in the sunlight, and I laughed and clapped with the other children. I knew the festivities were for May Day, and not for us, but I couldn't help but feel that it was a personal welcome to our new country. I was filled with hope and happiness, and I felt completely at home.

The day grew warm, and Doris showed me how to find the Lososinka River, where we all went wading and played on the riverbank. And then I dashed back to the Aronens' house, dirty, sunburned and happy. That afternoon my family moved into the room that was to be our home for the next two years. I think my mother was dismayed to find that we were given only one room for the five of us, but that was all anyone got when they first arrived. Housing had been a problem since the influx of foreigners had begun in 1930, and the town had never been able to keep up with the demand. My father assured her that the problem was only temporary, and he promised to start work on a house of our own just as soon as he could.

Our room was in a two-story wooden building at the corner of Lesnaya Ulitsa and Ulitsa Uritskovo. Ulitsa Uritskovo was one of the main streets of the city; it stretched the length of Petrozavodsk, ending at Lake Onega. The Lososinka River was not far from our room, just down the road, past a grove of trees and down a small

hill. Our building was called the Hotel because it was the first stop
for the American immigrants. They came here, stayed awhile, and
then moved on to logging communities up north or to cooperative
flats within Petrozavodsk.

But we were among the last of the immigrants; only one other
American family came to the Hotel after we did. There was no
need for us to move out of our room, since no one else was moving
in, and there was nowhere for us to move to, in any case.

Our room had a wood-burning stove for cooking, and we drew
water from a well in the yard. My mother did her best to make the
place homey. She strung up a curtain to divide the room in two.
In one half was the daybed that also served as a comfortable sofa;
in the other was a double bed, where Aino and I slept, and a big
steamer trunk that Paul curled up on at night. My mother hung
their wedding picture and a photo of my brother Leo on the bare
wall, unpacked the dishes and kitchen utensils, and that was our
home. It was spartan enough, but we were all willing to make
sacrifices for the good of the country. I don't remember anyone
complaining.

Paul liked the Hotel because of the long, narrow hallways; he
thought they were perfect for games of tag. On rainy afternoons
he would round up some of the other children who lived there and
bring them up to our floor, where they would scamper and race
up and down the hall, screaming with laughter and tagging each
other "it." Invariably, the game would end outside the door of
"Chewing Gum Martti"—Martti Hendrickson, the American
Communist leader, who lived across the hall from us. Hendrickson
had brought with him from America a nearly endless supply of
chewing gum, and it didn't take long for the children to find this
out. They would line up, squirming and giggling, outside his
room, and send one of the smallest and cutest kids to knock on
his door.

After a moment, the door would open, and Hendrickson—a
tall, serious man with a drooping mustache—would look down at

the small child. "Chewing gum?" the child would squeak, the other kids giggling behind.

Hendrickson would pause just long enough for the child to start doubting himself. Then he would grunt, "Uh huh," and disappear back into his room, reemerging a few seconds later with sticks of gum for all. I would often try to happen by casually at this point. I was too old and dignified to race up and down the hall, playing tag, but I wasn't too dignified to accept a piece of gum.

Most of the Finns stuck together here, as they had in America. For many of them, this was their second experience at emigration, and they were no longer young and adventurous. Most of the immigrants were middle-aged, with spouses and children, and I think it was difficult for them to learn a new language and adapt to a new culture. It's true that the Karelian language was similar to Finnish, but in Petrozavodsk most of the people spoke Russian. So the Finns opened their own Finnish-language school, put up a hall for Finnish concerts and plays, and didn't mix much with the Russian-speaking natives, other than to help them in their work.

I was placed in the fourth grade in the Finnish school, though I'd been in fifth grade in New York, and was told I'd better start boning up on my language skills if I wanted to catch up. Paul and Aino and I spoke only English to each other, and to Father; Father insisted on our English being perfect, and he corrected us whenever we made a mistake. But my mother still only understood Finnish. We spoke "Finglish" to her—a casual combination of Finnish and English that isn't real Finnish at all. We were dismayed to find that our Finglish was worthless here, and we would have to learn Finnish practically all over again.

Paul was placed in second grade, which he hated; he'd been in fourth grade in New York, and he was head and shoulders taller than the other students. But though he couldn't understand the language, he found his salvation in arithmetic. Languages change from country to country, but numbers are the same everywhere, and Paul began to excel in mathematics. To keep from falling too far behind in the other subjects, we both began swapping math tutoring for language tutoring.

From the moment we arrived in Petrozavodsk, Father was extremely busy. He donated his printing press to Kirja, a Finnish-language publishing house where he worked as an editor. He enrolled in night school to study Russian, and on Saturdays he and the other men donated their labor to the *subbotniks*—a volunteer labor force that met on Saturdays to build necessities for the city, such as housing, plumbing and sidewalks. He and three friends also started working on a big, two-story apartment house for our four families. They were following blueprints from America, and each apartment was to have three rooms and a kitchen. Mother was excited—in all of their married life, they had never owned their own home—and she talked quite often about how nice and roomy it would be once we could move. But between Father's job, his language lessons and the *subbotniks,* work on the house was often neglected, and its progress was slow. The needs of the community overshadowed the needs of individuals. That was the socialist way.

I didn't really mind the crowded quarters, and neither did Paul and Aino. We spent most of our time at school, anyway, or outside playing and watching the construction. It was exciting to see the town become transformed. Finns and Russians worked together building wooden pipes to draw water from Lake Onega and constructing buildings, roads and sidewalks around the town.

One day that fall, the Finns ran a boardwalk down our street. Paul and I went out early to watch, and someone handed him a hammer to help with the work, small as he was. I stood and watched as dozens of men came out of their homes to saw boards and pound nails. The work went quickly. The Finnish women stood on the doorsteps, wiping their hands on their aprons, shooing the children out of the way of the workers and chatting to each other over the tops of the men's heads.

Members of the Finnish youth orchestra turned out across the street to play tunes. Because they were so young, they were called the *Penikka Panti*, Finnish for "Puppy Band." They looked festive in their white flannel trousers and dark blazers. If only I had been able to get the hang of playing Leo's violin, I could have been playing with them, I thought. But though I loved music, I was quite content just to listen to the band and watch Paul pound nails. After that afternoon, we no longer had to walk in the mud.

Though the Finns tried to teach the Russians their skills and shared their tools, the two cultures just didn't mix well. The Russians weren't always receptive to having immigrants tell them how to improve their country, and most of the Finns didn't make an effort to assimilate. Many people, like my mother, didn't learn the Russian language. In all her time in the United States, my mother had never mastered English, and Russian was impossible for her; when she saw the alphabet, she just shook her head.

There were other annoyances, as well, for the Russians. We foreigners had ration cards that entitled us to shop at special stores for better food than the native Russians and Karelians could buy. One shop, "Insnab," was only for foreigners, and another shop, "Torgsin," accepted only hard currency, so those of us who still had dollars were able to buy things not generally available.

Many Americans had brought all kinds of things with them on the ships—sewing machines and wringer washers, pianos and automobiles. With our American clothes, American luxuries and ration cards, we must have evoked some envy in the Russian people. Life in Karelia was rough and difficult for us, but we still had privileges and possessions that most of the natives could only dream about.

I didn't really notice such subtle tensions; I was only a child. I don't even know if my parents were aware of them, though I assume my father was. He was studying the language, and he had more contact with the native Russians and Karelians than anyone else in the family. One young Karelian woman who lived in our building used to stop by and talk with him nearly every evening. I thought that her name was long and wonderful: Paraskeva Vasilyevena Lobskaya. I could barely pronounce it. She was a student at the Pedagogical Institute in town, and she was deeply interested in politics. Many nights she would stop by to discuss the philosophies of Marx and Lenin or current politics and no matter how tired Father was from his long day of work and his Russian lesson, he would make time for her. He truly believed that young people were the future of the country and needed to understand philosophy and ideology in order to be good citizens.

One morning during our first autumn there, as I danced along Lesnaya Street on my way to the store for my mother, I lost our monthly ration card in a sudden gust of wind. The wind stirred up the red and gold leaves around my feet and carried off the card so suddenly I stopped in amazement. It was mysterious—I looked and looked but couldn't find it, and I had to go home, head down, feet dragging, to confess.

My mother was worried that now we wouldn't have enough to eat, but Father said he was glad the card was gone. "We shouldn't have anything more than anyone else does," he said. "We are all Soviet citizens now, and we should all be treated the same." And he refused to apply for a new ration card.

All that month, we ate like Russians. We had cereal in the morning, usually with milk. My parents drank lots of tea—coffee was hard to come by, but the strong, hot tea was always in good supply. We had no fresh fruits or vegetables, but there was always bread and potatoes, and some kind of meat once or twice a week. My mother was a creative cook; she could concoct a wonderful, nourishing soup out of a handful of potatoes and very little else. We didn't eat fancy food, but we never went hungry.

That first winter was one of the coldest I had ever experienced. The cook stove heated our room fairly well, but we had to feed the fire constantly, and even when the stove glowed red-hot we could sometimes feel the wind howling through the thin walls of our room. Our well froze over, and every morning we broke through the ice to draw water for washing and cooking. Any water we spilled froze so quickly that after a few days the well was nearly encased in ice, like a frozen fountain, and Father and the other men had to come out and chop it free with an axe.

In New York we had had a separate laundry room, equipped with a wringer washer and plenty of soap, hot water and galvanized laundry tubs. But here, of course, we didn't have those things, and we had to learn how to wash our clothes the Russian way. The first time we tried, the laundry took the better part of a day, though later we grew more skillful.

First we heated the water in a big boiler on our wood stove and then scrubbed the clothes on a washboard. The windows fogged over, and my mother's wavy hair curled around her face in the steamy heat. Either Paul or I would always help. We would pull on our boots and mittens and wrap long scarves around our heads, and then load the wet clothes into a huge woven basket, which we dragged out the door and put on our sled. Mother cut a long stick from one of the trees across the way, and we pulled the sled down to the banks of the Lososinka River. Our mittens were damp from handling the wet clothes, and they became stiff with ice almost instantly. There were other people down at the riverside doing their washing as well, twirling the clothes expertly onto their sticks and dunking the laundry among the ice chunks. I watched them, my breath coming out of my mouth in little puffs of steam, until my scarf frosted over and stuck to my face.

My mother did her best to imitate the others. She took the stick and picked up one of the dripping sheets with it, twirling the stick to wind the sheet around it securely. The heavy, wet sheet flapped in the cold air, and it took both her hands to hold onto the stick. Then she dunked it in the river again and again to rinse it. Once or twice she lost a piece of clothing and had to poke around for it in the icy river water. It wouldn't do to lose anything, because clothes and fabric were so hard to come by.

One by one, she rinsed the sheets and clothes and slid them off the stick into the woven basket. The basket had big holes in the bottom so the water could drain out, but on cold days the water froze quickly. Together, my mother and I took the rope in our mittened hands and dragged the sled slowly back up the hill to the Hotel. Everything was so sodden and icy that the sled felt twice as heavy as it had before. By the time we got home, most of the laundry was frozen solid, and Mother went inside and heated more water, which she poured over the clothes to thaw them. And then she and I fed them through the wringer, one at a time, and hung them on the line to freeze dry.

After that, we pulled off our wet things, rubbed our hands together over the stove until they tingled, and had a good steaming cup of tea.

This is how we lived for two years: all in one room, washing our clothes in the river, eating Russian food and almost never getting anything new—no clothes or books or toys. The stores just didn't carry much of anything, and we didn't have much money to spare.

In early December of our first winter in Petrozavodsk, I came home from school one day to see my parents looking grim and frightened. Sergei Kirov, one of the most trusted Communist party members in all of the Soviet Union, had been assassinated in Leningrad.

"Assassinated!" my mother said, twisting her hands in her apron. "It's so hard to believe, Oscar! He was such a good man! Who would have wanted him dead?"

My father just shook his head.

Kirov was the Leningrad party secretary, a close friend of Josef Stalin and a popular leader. He had remained a man of the people, despite his rise to power, and had worked hard to improve the living conditions in Leningrad and to promote factory production and agriculture. He had been shot dead in the afternoon of December 1, 1934, as he left his Leningrad office for the day. News of his death was reported in *Pravda*, the Communist party newspaper, and the story was rimmed with a wide black border.

That evening, some of Father's friends came by our room after Paul, Aino and I were in bed. Through the curtain, I could hear Kalle Aronen, Martti Hendrickson, Vaino Finberg and other prominent American Communists talking late into the night about Kirov's death and what it meant. I couldn't understand why they sounded so grave—I knew that the man's death was tragic, but it seemed to me that his murder must have been the act of some lone lunatic. Still, I lay in the dark and listened, as I used to do in my bed back in Superior.

"They've arrested a half-dozen men in Leningrad on counter-revolutionary charges," Aronen said. "And they say there are more arrests to come."

"What evidence do they have?" my father asked.

Aronen snorted. "They don't tell us these things," he said. "The same evidence they had when they arrested those fellows last week, I expect."

And then my mother's voice, whispered, worried: "Please! Keep it down! The children are sleeping!" But I somehow felt that it wasn't just us she worried about.

A few months later my father was called to Moscow by Yrjo Sirola, the Finnish Marxist he had first met in America. Sirola had moved to the Soviet Union years ago and now worked for Comintern, the international Communist organization. This was the second time Sirola had summoned my father, the first being just a few months after we arrived.

After three days in Moscow, Father came home. Mother ran to greet him as he took off his hat and hung it on a peg inside the door. "What did he want with you?" she asked, helping him off with his overcoat. "Such an important man!"

My father glanced around to see if any of us were within earshot.

I bent over my schoolbooks and pretended not to listen. "He said the same thing that he said last summer," my father said, lowering his voice. I strained to hear him. "He said there are bad times ahead. He suggested I take all of you and go back to the United States."

My mother sank down in a chair. "Bad times? What does he mean?" she asked, her hand over her mouth. My father didn't answer. "What did you tell him?" she asked.

There was a long pause. "I told him I couldn't do that," he said finally, and I peeked to see my mother's face. She was watching my father steadily, nodding in agreement. "I told him that I brought hundreds of American Finns over here, and I'm not leaving unless I can take all of them back with me," he said.

"Of course you're right," my mother said. "Of course we'll stay. And how bad can things get, anyway? We're making progress here every day."

That night, Hendrickson, Aronen, Finberg and Tenhunen came again and sat up until long after I was asleep. They discussed the mysterious message of Yrjo Sirola and what it might mean. My mother hustled us off to bed as soon as they arrived, even though it was still early, and she pulled the curtain as tightly as she could. But as I drifted off to sleep, I could still hear their voices, worried and confused, uncertain murmurs in the dark.

Wanting to Belong

I awoke to the sun sparkling off the frosted windows and a new carpet of thick white snow outside. I threw back the covers, thoughts of skating filling my head. The wooden floor was cold, and I scampered out to the other side of the curtain to warm myself at the stove. My mother was gathering up the teacups that were scattered around from the night before, reminders that my father's friends had been there again and had stayed until quite late. More and more often, his American Communist friends came by at night to talk urgently in whispered Finnish about mysterious reports coming out of Moscow. This happened so often now that I didn't listen as much as I used to. I didn't really understand their concerns, and I wasn't as interested as I used to be. I was beginning to develop a life of my own.

In my eyes, Petrozavodsk had begun to thrive. The Finns had brought more than machinery and equipment with them; they had also brought knowledge and culture. For a backward town deep in the forest of Soviet Karelia, there were soon a lot of wonderful things going on. There was a brass band and a symphony orchestra, both made up almost entirely of Finns. Many of the musicians were old friends of mine from America. Ruth Niskanen took up the violin. Sirkka Rikka, a dramatic young woman with raven hair and a pure, golden voice, began singing on the radio. And Milton Sevander from Eveleth, Minnesota, also joined the orchestra. He came from a theatrical family; his father, Kuuno, was already a well-known singer in the United States and Finland, and his uncle, Kalle, was an actor in Petrozavodsk. Milton had smiling blue eyes and a ready laugh and was one of the best trombone players I had ever heard.

My mother, who loved music, often said that the Karelian Radio Symphony Orchestra in Petrozavodsk was one of the finest orchestras she had ever heard. I think she was proud of the fact that most of the musicians were American Finns. Workers had put up a beautiful philharmonic concert hall with perfect acoustics, and my friends and I started going to concerts every chance we got. Mother seldom had time to attend, but she would put on the radio in the evenings and listen to the concerts while she did the mending. She always said that listening to the cheerful folk music and beautiful classical pieces made it easy to forget for a few minutes that our walls were rough, our food poor and our feet cold.

The Finns had also started a theater, where many of my parents' friends began working. Otto Bjorninen, a kindly-faced Finn who had come here from Bessemer, Michigan, lived near us. Otto was an actor, and his young son Orvo, had already started following him to the theater. And the actors Aarne and Irja Nieminen lived on the floor below us at the Hotel. They were a fun-loving young couple, newly married, and sometimes I could hear them pacing the floor of their tiny room, reciting their lines and laughing.

My mother's play-acting days were behind her now; she had performed in plays long ago at the Finn halls in Hancock and Superior, but she no longer had the time to do that here. "Oh, leave that to the young folk," she used to say. But she never lost her love of the theater, and now and again she would take us all to the Finnish Theater to see one of the classic Russian or Finnish plays performed there. I loved to sit in my wooden seat at the theater and smell the musty curtain and see everyone around me, dressed up and expectant as the lights fell low. When I saw Aarne Nieminen on the stage, I had to remind myself that I knew him, that he was our neighbor, because with his stage makeup and his acting skills, he always became whatever character he portrayed. My mother would watch closely, leaning forward slightly in her seat, her lips parted, and I wondered if she was remembering her own days on the stage.

Sometimes the Nieminens were gone for several days or weeks at a time; the Finnish Theater often went on the road to some of the little logging settlements in the countryside, to entertain the workers at Matrosa and Kondopoga and other towns. In the winter of 1936, they were gone for an entire month, skiing from town to town and carrying their costumes and sets on their backs. A whole group of them went, and I remember how excited they were when they got back. Mother and Father had the Nieminens up for a cup of tea, and they talked far into the night about how thrilled the loggers were to see them and what a success their performances had been.

That winter I learned to ice skate, and Paul fell in love with cross-country skiing. The Finns had started a ski factory where they built the most beautiful wooden cross-country skis, and on crisp January afternoons Paul would strap on his skis and disappear for hours, gliding for miles among the birch and pine trees that lined the bank of the frozen Lososinka River.

The skating, skiing, and music and theater were wonderful ways to make the long, dark winter days speed by. But there was something else, too, that made our early life in Soviet Karelia so special: a spirit that I had never felt before or since, a spirit of cooperation and humanity. It's hard to explain without sounding sentimental, but as my brother said years later, "People were different then. They were better." And, in a way, they were. There was a sincerity, a common goal. You never got the feeling that anyone was in it just for himself, or was trying to make a profit at someone else's expense. It was the spirit of socialism, though the streets were muddy and the stores often bare.

And they certainly were bare. During the two years we lived in the Hotel, the stores stocked fewer and fewer goods. We never understood it; we American Finns were improving the town and helping Karelia to increase its timber production and meet the goals of its five-year plan, but for some reason the economy wasn't improving. By 1936, ration cards were outlawed, and immigrants were left to shop at the Russian stores. The "Insnab" store closed down, and "Torgsin" remained only for those lucky people who still had dollars, silver or gold stashed away, which my family certainly didn't.

Credit dried up. My father and his friends could no longer get materials and had to quit working on our apartment house. They had poured the basement, but without credit they couldn't buy what they needed to build the walls—if, indeed, those materials were even available.

And though the economy was certainly equalizing us all, we Finns were still living separately, attending our own schools and socializing at the halls. To me, this made no sense. We had moved to this country, and if we were ever going to fit in, we needed to learn the language. So when the school year began in the fall of 1936, I asked my parents if I could leave the Finnish school and enroll in one of the Russian schools. I had learned a few phrases from the Russian girls I played with, but I had a long way to go before I would be fluent. And I truly wanted to be fluent. This was my home; my father had brought me here, and I knew I was bound to stay here for the rest of my life. I wanted to fit in; I didn't want to be like my mother, an immigrant forever. I wanted to belong.

My father understood immediately. He had been studying Russian for more than a year, and while he could already read the newspapers fairly well, he knew that my young mind would pick up the language much more quickly than he had.

So that fall, while Paul and Aino walked off together each morning to the Finnish school, I walked off in another direction, alone, to the Russian school, where I knew almost no one and where I couldn't communicate at all. Two of my American friends, Inga Honka and Ruth Merila, had made the same decision. They were older than I and in a different class, but it was still comforting to see familiar faces in the hallway.

The Russian school was a new brick building, which had big clean classrooms with tall windows that let in lots of sunlight. It was a cheerful enough place, but many mornings I headed off to school with my feet dragging and a feeling of dread in the pit of my stomach. It was in the Russian school that I first encountered Ludmila Ivanovna Bogdanova, who I thought must be the strictest teacher in the world. She was very stout and had a forbidding walk, a slow *clomp-clomp-clomp* that struck fear into the hearts of all students who hadn't done their homework. It struck fear into my heart too, for though I did my homework diligently, I just couldn't get the hang of Russian.

My first dictation assignment was a disaster. I worked so hard on it, sitting up half the night while my family slept, going over and over the spelling by the light of a single lamp. It was a miracle that I finished it at all. I handed it in the next day with a mingled feeling of accomplishment and dread.

Ludmila Ivanovna handed my paper back the next day. She trudged slowly over to my desk to present it to me in front of the entire class. My paper contained, she said in her rich theatrical voice, no fewer than 168 errors. And she had taken the time to correct them all.

I saved that assignment for years, that piece of paper swimming in red ink. Looking at it made me grit my teeth and vow to go on. I had a strong feeling that she wanted me to quit, and later I found out that my feeling was right: I got wind of the fact that after my first few weeks in her class she asked the principal to expel me. She thought I was an ignorant Finn who was bringing down the quality of the class by bogging her down in elementary questions that any Russian child of five would understand. But I was not to be beaten.

I studied Russian every chance I got. I brought the books home with me. I pored over them in the evening; I tried to snatch a moment to read over breakfast in the morning. I went from being an indifferent straight-A student in the Finnish school to being the most diligent, hard-working scholar I could imagine. I never doubted that I would learn the language, but I wished it wouldn't take so long. And day after day, Ludmila Ivanovna handed back my red-marked papers and glared at me.

At the end of my first term in the Russian school, I received my grades: All 2's—the Russian equivalent of D's—except for math, music and physical education, where language wasn't as important. I couldn't believe it. I had tried so hard, worked so diligently, and I was on the verge of failing. All the courses were taught in Russian, and the textbooks for all the courses were in Russian, as well, so until I could master the language, I knew that none of my grades were going to get much better.

I was deep in the second term of Russian when my father came home one day with an important announcement. The publishing house was transferring him to Uhtua, a small Finnish-speaking town up north. I didn't say anything right away. Everyone else was delighted; my mother's face brightened when Father told her that we would finally have a small house to ourselves. "We could have a garden!" she said, smiling broadly. "Oh, Oscar, we can have our own tomatoes and cucumbers and—just think, fresh lettuce!"

Everyone in Uhtua spoke Finnish, and I knew my mother would feel much more at home there. For her, it would almost be like being back in Finland again.

Paul, too, was glad. Petrozavodsk had a lot to offer, but he was, at heart, a country boy. Uhtua was deep in the wilderness, where he could ski for miles in solitude, snare rabbits for dinner, and fish for salmon and trout, like the grandfather in Sweden that he had never met. I could see him plotting, already, how to make a fishing pole and figuring out where he might find some string that would do for line.

And Aino was so young that she was happy to go anywhere.

Only I remained silent. I was thirteen now, and I knew that if I moved to Uhtua, my chances of mastering Russian and fitting into this new country would be diminished. Russian was hard, but I knew I'd catch on eventually. And I had many good friends— both Finns and Russians—whom I didn't want to leave. I was old enough to go out alone now, and once or twice a week my friends would come by to get me and we'd go to the movies, a concert or one of the plays at the Finnish theater. We knew all the musicians and actors, and we always went backstage afterwards and then out for ice cream or tea. I felt at home here in Petrozavodsk, and I didn't want to be uprooted once again.

My father noticed my silence and asked me what I was thinking. I swallowed hard and told him the truth: "I don't want to go," I said. I could see disappointment spreading across my mother's face, but I had to go on. "I want to stay here and learn Russian," I said. "Don't you think I could stay behind? Just for the school year?" I decided it best not to mention that I also didn't want to leave my friends; that reason didn't sound quite as noble.

My father looked very serious. I was still so young, and since Leo's death I knew he wanted to keep the family together as long as possible. But I could also tell he thought that what I said made sense. He didn't answer right away.

But my mother did. "Oh, Mayme, of course you're coming!" she said. "We can't do without you! Surely you can take up your Russian studies again later."

I looked at my father. I knew that my mother would miss me, her eldest daughter and her helper, and she would worry about me, so far away from the rest of the family. But I trusted my father to make the right decision.

He looked me straight in the eye, and I stood in front of him and looked straight back. I tried to look as mature and responsible as possible. And then he smiled. "All right," he said, nodding. "If you can find a place to live, you can stay. But you'll come and live with us in Uhtua when school is out in the spring."

I think he was proud of my request. He understood my need to become part of the country. He would miss me, too, but he wasn't going to stand in the way of my education.

They left Petrozavodsk in January of 1937. I was sorry to see my family go, but I was sure I had made the right decision. My father left first, to get settled, and I made plans to move across the hall of the Hotel to live in the one-room apartment of my schoolmate, Miriam Kupiainen, and her mother, Hilda. It was just the two of them there; Miriam's father was in Finland. He was one of many people who had been surprised and discouraged at the harsh conditions he found here, and he had fled the Soviet Union soon after arriving.

But his wife and daughter were unable to go with him. Like hundreds of other hopeful, idealistic immigrants, Miriam and Hilda had willingly surrendered their American passports to the Soviet authorities upon arrival. Now, without a foreign passport, they could not leave the country. It was a hard, lonely life for them, and I think they were glad for my companionship.

I knew that Miriam's father wasn't alone in leaving, though it was hard to understand how he could leave his family behind. In the last two years, as conditions here had grown harder, many more American Finns had abandoned the socialist dream and returned home. The group we had encountered in Sweden was not unusual; perhaps as many as half of the estimated six thousand people who came from North America changed their minds and left soon after they arrived.

I didn't really understand it; of course it was a hard life, but we had known that it would be hard even before we came. Without ration cards the food was scarce, and living in one room certainly was a cramped way to get along, but socialists weren't supposed to be materialistic, and even I could see that we had already made a difference here. And that made me proud.

I didn't talk to Miriam about her father; she and her mother had welcomed me into their life to share what they had, and I was grateful. So on a cold afternoon I moved my things into their room, and my mother, brother and sister left town. I saw them off at the station, where they caught the train to Kem, a port town on the White Sea. From there, they planned to take a bus for the 182-kilometer trip to Uhtua.

Paul told me later what it was like. They arrived in Uhtua late at night, he said, after an endless, bone-jarring bus ride along slippery winter roads. It was a bitter cold, black night, with the stars above them just bright dots of light. All they could see of the town was one light burning in the distance. They climbed off the bus and huddled in their scarves and big coats, stomping their numb feet on the hard, squeaky snow.

Father met them there. He had found them a nice little wooden house right on the banks of the river, and the wood stove was glowing a red-hot welcome for them when they arrived, chilled to the bone, but home.

Father worked in a bookstore as a representative of Kirja Publishing, and Mother soon found a job in an orphanage. Paul entered the fourth grade, and Aino started second grade. They all seemed happier than they had been in a long time. Two years in that single room in the Hotel had taken their toll, and though my family never fought, they were weary of such close quarters. In Uhtua, they had more space, more freedom.

Their letters made me miss them, but I knew that it wouldn't be long until summer, when I could move to Uhtua, too.

Meanwhile, I was continuing my daily battle with the biggest challenge I had ever faced: the Russian language, as taught by Ludmila Ivanovna.

Day after day Ludmila Ivanovna handed me back my red-scrawled assignments, and day after day I was in despair. But I plugged away, determined to make sense of this complicated language. It was so unlike English, so unlike Finnish, but I was beginning to see that it also had a beautiful, rich sound and an emotional vibrancy that appealed to me. I knew I would like it if I could ever come to understand it.

In early spring, my mother came down for a visit. I was glad to see her; she brought me money, some lovely printed fabric for a new dress and, best of all, news from the family.

"Paul found a white cat somewhere, it follows him everywhere, like a dog, but I think it's deaf," she said, linking her arm in mine as we walked along the windy street. "Aino has a new best friend, a Karelian girl who lives not far away. And your father is very busy, of course. I'm planning my garden. I think the season is too short for tomatoes, but I'm going to try them anyway, and potatoes and cucumbers and onions and lettuce."

She seemed so cheerful and happy to see me that I was afraid to ruin her mood by talking about school. So when she asked me how my Russian studies were going, I told her that all was well. She came to school with me the next morning, and I introduced her to Ludmila Ivanovna.

"Your daughter cannot learn the language," Ludmila Ivanovna told my mother immediately. She was never one to mince words. "You might as well take her back home with you to Uhtua."

"What is she saying?" my mother asked me. Thank goodness my mother couldn't understand Russian! So I translated: "She said I'm making good progress," I said.

My mother smiled at Ludmila Ivanovna. "You must be an excellent teacher," she said. "Thank you for working with my daughter."

"What is she saying?" Ludmila Ivanovna asked. Thank goodness she couldn't understand Finnish! Again, I translated. "She begs you to give me a little more time," I said.

"Tell her you will never learn the language!" Ludmila Ivanovna thundered.

"Yes, I'm glad she is working so hard," said my mother.

"Nyet! Nyet! Nyet!" Ludmila Ivanovna said. She was beginning to understand that she had lost control of the conversation.

"Why is she saying 'Nyet'?" asked my mother. "Doesn't that mean 'No'?"

"She's saying she doesn't want me to leave," I said.

My mother rose and smiled at Ludmila Ivanovna. "I'm glad my Mayme is doing so well in your school," she said, shaking the teacher's hand in farewell. "Thank you so much for all you have done."

And I walked my mother back to the train station.

After that I knew I'd better study Russian harder than ever. My next assignment was to read Gogol's "Inspector General" in the original Russian and then retell it in class. Miriam was still attending the Finnish school and wasn't much help, but I told the story out loud to her and her mother, anyway, as we did the dishes. They couldn't understand a word of Russian, but they were quite impressed. Her mother kept smiling and saying, "You're so smart, Mayme! Just listen to her, Miriam!" But I knew that my Russian was only impressive to those who didn't know the language. I told them that story ten different ways; I told it all night long. The next morning I was filled with confidence. Today would be the day, I felt sure, that I would finally impress Ludmila Ivanovna.

When she began calling on students for recitation, my hand shot up in the air. She looked at me curiously and raised one eyebrow. "Well, Mayme Corgan thinks she can do it," she said. "Shall we give her a try?" And she looked at me with such a cold expression that I was filled with dread.

I rose slowly and closed my book. I stood by my desk, trembling. I shifted my weight from foot to foot. I opened my mouth, but no words came out.

The class was silent. Thirty-two Russian children, and one large

Russian woman, stared at me. I stood there a while longer, and then I sat down.

"You see?" said Ludmila Ivanovna, a note of triumph in her voice. "You don't do your homework. You don't know Russian. You will never know Russian."

The tears rushed into my eyes. I had never cried easily, but the frustration of trying so hard and being so far away from my family and working so diligently, night after night, in vain, spilled over and the tears streamed down my face.

"I did my homework!" I said. "I tried very hard!" Ludmila Ivanovna just looked at me. I swallowed and said, "Can I stay after class and recite it to you in private?"

She shrugged. "All right," she said, and called on another student.

At the end of the day, I stopped at her desk. She looked up at me. "Yes?" she asked. She seemed to have forgotten why I was there. I took a deep breath and launched into my retelling of Gogol's story. It wasn't perfect, and somehow it didn't sound nearly as impressive as it had the night before in Miriam's room, but I got it all out. I told the story and then I stood there at her desk, breathing hard.

"Well," she said, and put down her pencil. I waited. "I see you have done your homework," she said. I waited. And then she nodded. "I see I was wrong. You have tried. Well, I'm sorry I misjudged you. Keep it up." And she picked up her pencil and bent over her papers again.

I floated out of the classroom. That nod! It was almost friendly! And an apology! Suddenly I understood that Ludmila Ivanovna was no demon. She was a teacher—a teacher with high standards and a love of learning, a teacher for whom I wanted to work hard and whose respect I vowed to earn. The thought occurred to me that perhaps I might be such a teacher some day myself.

The third term ended. I received satisfactory marks in everything, and I was doing better in Russian. The last term ended. My marks had risen even further. I was doing well in everything, and—miracle of miracles—I had managed a 4, a "B," in Russian. When school let out for the summer, I boarded the train to Uhtua with a cheerful heart. I had worked hard and sacrificed, like a good socialist, and now I was going home to my family.

They Took My Father

The sun was not yet up, but I could hear Paul sneaking out of bed.

"Paul, where are you going?" I asked in a whisper. Aino still slept quietly beside me.

"Fishing," he said, tiptoeing across the wooden floor. Mother had washed it the night before in honor of my homecoming, scrubbed it bone-white with sand from the riverside, and a few stray grains skittered across his path. "Do you want to come along with me?"

I threw back the blankets and pulled my dress on over my head. "I'll watch," I said. I wasn't really interested in sitting on the riverbank and waiting for hours for a fish to bite, but I did want to explore a little before it was time to help my mother with breakfast.

It was a clear morning in June. School was behind me, Ludmila Ivanovna was behind me, the noise and bustle of a growing Petrozavodsk were behind me, and there was nothing ahead but three months vacation to spend with my family in the lovely Karelian countryside. I had come into Uhtua late the night before, traveling the whole way with a group of actors from the Petroza-vodsk Finnish Theater. During the long journey by train from Petrozavodsk to Kem, and then the eternal bus trip from Kem to Uhtua, they entertained me with jokes and songs and anecdotes about life on the stage. They were a cheerful, lively bunch and I was glad to hear they planned to spend several weeks in Uhtua, bringing theater to the people.

It was late when we arrived, and all I could see of the town were a few small houses and many tall trees, black shapes against the night sky. So the next morning, as I followed Paul through the tall, scratchy grass down to the rocky riverbank, I looked around with interest. Uhtua was just a little village, a sprinkling of tiny log homes amidst tall pines.

"I come here every morning," he said. "I almost always catch something." Just as Mother had said, his white cat followed him down to the riverbank and stretched in the sun, yawning.

I dangled my bare feet in the water—the river was surprisingly cold, and very clear—and watched Paul bait his hook with a wriggling worm.

"How do you like it here?" I asked him.

"I like it," he said. "I go fishing every day. That's all I want out of life. And I led the class in math last term. Are you glad you stayed behind?"

I sighed. "Russian was hard," I said. "It's much harder than Finnish. But I think I'm doing the right thing. And Miriam and her mother seem glad to have me there."

Paul got a nibble, a small fish that chewed on his worm and then swam away in a swirl of bubbles. He hauled in his line and put a fresh worm on the hook. "Something's going on here," he said, scowling as he tended to the worm. "I'm not sure exactly what, but Mother and Father seem worried."

"What do you mean?" I asked.

"Some of the men are gone," he said. "The fathers of some of my friends. Someone said they were arrested."

"Arrested!" I said. "What for? What have they done?"

"I don't think they did anything," said Paul.

We sat silently for a long time. I felt a sudden chill and pulled my feet from the water and curled them up underneath me, but it took a long time to get warm.

Finally, Paul pulled in his line again. "Let's go see if Mother needs us to get some water," he said. "It must be time for breakfast."

That summer passed by in a whirl of sunshine and laughter. I helped my mother with her garden. It was nice to have lettuce salad again, and fresh cucumbers. Her tomatoes did produce, though not all of them turned red, and she spent a few afternoons making green tomato pickles. I got up early each morning and helped her with breakfast before she hurried off to her job at the orphanage. Aino and I washed the dishes and swept the floor, and then we were free for the day.

For such a small town, Uhtua had a large number of young people, and we all gathered at the river for sunbathing and swimming. In the evenings, sometimes, there were dances. We stayed up late during the "white nights" of June and early July when the sun disappeared for only a few hours around midnight.

I had grown taller over the winter, and now that it was summer, the Karelian sun bleached out my blonde hair. Though I was barely into my teens, there suddenly seemed to be quite a number of boys hanging around our house and following my friends and me to the river. One of them, an actor from Petrozavodsk, was particularly persistent and seemed to be at our house every time I turned around. My father took it all with good humor, but he was also strict, and every now and then he would lose patience and send the young man home again.

Father was quite impressed by the strides I had made in learning Russian, and sometimes he would have me read aloud to him from the Russian newspaper. Uhtua was only thirty kilometers from the

Finnish border, and everything there was in Finnish—the newspaper, the books in the bookstore, the classes at school. But Father had saved some copies of the Petrozavodsk Russian-language paper and liked to read them over and over, for practice.

It was one evening when I was reading aloud to him that I found out that Kustaa Rovio and Edvard Gylling, the two leaders of Soviet Karelia, had been arrested several months before. "What for?" I asked.

Father frowned. "Nationalism," he said. "That's what the papers say. Enemies of the people."

"What does that mean?" I asked.

My father shook his head. "It's not for you to worry about," he said. "They must have done something that we don't know about. But I thought they were good men."

I put it out of my mind. Granted, they had been good leaders and they had been instrumental in bringing all of us American Finns to Karelia, but politics were a mystery to me. You just never knew why things happened, or what secret things people might have done.

The days flowed by, one golden week melting into the next, and all too soon I began awakening to an autumn chill in the air. The leaves had started to turn, starbursts of red and gold among the green, and I knew it was time to head back to Petrozavodsk, and to school.

My mother wept when I boarded the bus for Kem, where I would catch the Petrozavodsk train. "Be careful, Mayme," she said, pressing bundles of garden vegetables into my arms. "We'll miss you. Study hard."

My father gathered me in a tight embrace. I pressed my face against his chest and breathed in the familiar, homey smells: the smell of printers ink, of wool, of the clean dirt from the family garden and the warm scent of tobacco from the Lucky Strikes that he smoked on rare occasions. I wanted to remember those odors, that comforting scent of family, hold it in my lungs until I could come back to Uhtua and see them all again.

I climbed onto the bus, laden with bags and packages and bundles, and found my way to my seat. Through the grimy bus window, I waved at my parents to let them know I was settled. The square shape of the window made a perfect picture frame for my family as they stood together by the side of the road, and I tried to memorize how they all looked at that moment—my father, tall and dignified, his dark hair sprinkled with the beginnings of gray; my mother, grown a little stoutish, but still with those lovely brown eyes; Aino and Paul, looking cheerful and rumpled and sunburned. I waved and waved as the bus took off, jolting down the rutted road, spewing blue exhaust, and I kept on waving until they were out of sight.

Winter came early that year. On a stormy day in November, I hurried home along the darkened sidewalk, my scarf wrapped round and round my face and my head bent into the wind. If summer meant white nights and parties, winter meant dark days of overcast skies and strong winds that whipped my coat as I trudged to and from school.

I was wondering what we would have for dinner that night (Mother had sent some canned vegetables home with me, but by the end of October we had eaten most of them), and I was hoping that dinner wouldn't be just potatoes and bread again. So many other things were rationed, or just impossible to find. Thank goodness there was always plenty of hot, sweet tea. I turned in the walkway of the Hotel and noticed Hilda's face pressed against the window, looking out at me.

"Mayme, there's been someone here to see you. A woman," she said, before I could even unwind my scarf and sit down. "She says she's from Uhtua, and she has some sort of message from your mother. She was very eager to see you. She said to tell you she's staying with friends at the house next door."

"Oh, yes!" I said. I was glad to hear about any visitor from Uhtua. Mother and Father often sent me money, clothing and— sometimes—canned goods with visitors who were on their way to Petrozavodsk. If I were really lucky, there'd be a jar of green tomato pickles, or one of beets from my mother's garden, and we could have a wonderful dinner. It was getting close to the November holidays, so I was sure my mother would have sent along some kind of surprise.

I buttoned up my coat and went back out into the bitter wind to find the woman from Uhtua. But when I found her, she barely greeted me.

"What do you have for me?" I asked. "Did they send money?"

She stared at me, and I was surprised to see that she was trembling. "I have a letter for you," she said. "But there is no money. There is no gift."

My face fell. "No gift?" I asked, taking the letter. And suddenly the woman began to cry. I had never seen anyone cry like that, huge sobs that shook her whole body.

"Mayme," she gasped. "I have such terrible news for you. There's been a great misfortune."

A cold fear spread inside me and I couldn't speak. I waited for her to continue. "Your father," she said, and I went pale. "Your father has been taken away."

My knees buckled, and I looked around wildly for somewhere to sit down. She put her arms around me, but I pushed her away. "What do you mean?" I demanded. "What do you mean my father has been taken away?"

"He's been arrested," she said. She was still crying, and her voice came out in little gasps. "I'm sure it's all a misunderstanding. I'm sure that he'll be home again soon. Your mother says that you mustn't worry."

I tore open the letter to read the news in my mother's own words. Between her letter and what Paul told me later, this is what I learned.

They came in the night—there were two of them. One was our neighbor, Mr. Kiuru, a good Finnish man. Late on the night of November 4, 1937, they knocked on the door, waking my family. They told Father that he was under arrest and would have to go with them. They wouldn't answer any questions. They left the door open, letting the cold night wind blow into the front room. Aino held tightly onto my mother's skirts, terrified, and Paul stood next to her like a little protector. The men wouldn't answer any of their questions.

The men searched the house, looking for who knows what. They took our radio, our camera, Father's typewriter, all our papers and birth certificates from America, the leatherbound notebooks that Father was saving for our college days, and most of our photo albums. No one knew why. No one knew what they wanted.

Father told Mother not to worry. He said he'd get this straightened out and would be back before she knew it.

The men let him dress, but as he was putting his gold watch into his vest pocket, Mr. Kiuru stopped him. "You leave that watch at home with your family, Oscar," he said. "It's better that you leave it at home."

Father just looked at him and then slowly set the watch back down on the table. "Paul," he said, his voice breaking the terrible silence that filled the house. "Can I borrow your watch?" And Paul gave him his old stainless steel watch to take.

My father strapped Paul's watch onto his wrist, and the two men led him away. The wooden front door banged behind them, and they were gone. That was all. They were gone.

I finished reading my mother's letter and crumpled it into my pocket. The woman from Uhtua tried to speak to me, but I turned from her and ran. I ran out the door, down the steps and up the sidewalk, straight into the wind. I ran past pedestrians in the street, who turned and stared. I ran until my lungs ached and my feet felt leaden from my heavy winter boots. I ran until I could no longer breathe. I ran until I found myself at the room of my friend, Vieno Sevander, and when she opened her door I pushed past her and threw myself on her bed.

That's when I began to cry.

I cried so hard I couldn't speak, and Vieno became frightened and called in her father from outside, where he was having a smoke. Kalle Sevander sat down on one side of me, and Vieno sat on the other, and they begged me to tell them what was wrong.

But when I told them, choking out the words between tears and gasps, Kalle's response filled me with anger.

"You know, Mayme, they don't arrest innocent people," he said softly. "I'm sorry that your father has been taken away. Nobody respects Oscar Corgan more than I do. But you don't know, really, what's happened. Your father has traveled so much, and he's been involved for so long in international movements. How do you know? Maybe he got entangled with something he shouldn't have."

Kalle Sevander was my friend, and his daughter was my friend, but I could not let that pass. I sat up, tears staining my face, my hair and clothes rumpled. "My father has done nothing wrong," I said coldly. "My father is an honorable and sincere man."

"They don't arrest innocent people," Kalle said again. "But if your father is innocent, you have nothing to worry about. They will send him home again soon." And he patted my head and left the room.

That was the longest winter of my young life. In his parting words to my mother, my father had said I should stay in Petrozavodsk and continue my schooling, so I did. I wrote desperate letters home to my mother, begging for information, but there was no information to give.

My mother was beside herself. She wrote to everyone, trying to find out what had happened to my father, why he'd been taken, where he'd been taken, when he was coming home. No one would tell her. No one knew.

And suddenly, it was happening everywhere. Not a night went by when there wasn't a knock on a door somewhere in Uhtua, somewhere in Petrozavodsk, somewhere in Kondopoga, and they would take away another man, another good Finn, another loyal socialist, another loving father and husband.

They took Otto Bjorinen, the kindly actor. No one knew why.

They took Vaino Finberg, one of the most steadfast Communists there was. No one knew why.

They took Antti Nissinen, the Red Finn who was married to my Aunt Maria. No one knew why.

One morning half of the symphony orchestra didn't show up for rehearsal. They had all been arrested. No one knew why.

One morning only three people from a team of twenty showed up at the ski factory. The other seventeen had been taken away. And no one knew why.

Irja and Aarne, the actors on the first floor, had just had a child, but the men came in the night for Aarne anyway. We heard the knock after midnight. We heard Irja's sobs.

One afternoon she came to Hilda and Miriam and me with her infant son wrapped in a blanket. "Can you watch him for me?" she asked. Her face was thin and she had dark circles under her beautiful blue eyes. "I must find out what happened to Aarne. I'm going to talk to the police. I will be back."

And they took her away, too.

Months went by. We watched her baby, whom we nicknamed little Pokko, grow and learn to hold up his head and roll over and push himself up on his little hands and knees. Still she didn't come back, and her husband didn't come back. And they continued to arrest people.

They took away Olavi Siikki, one of the actors who had skied all month to bring theater to the settlements.

They took away Kalle Sevander. His last words to his wife and daughter were, "Tell Mayme I now believe that her father was innocent."

They took my friends' fathers and sometimes my friends' mothers; they took shopkeepers and musicians and actors and workers and teachers and men who swept the streets.
And no one knew why.

And they took my father. They took my father. They took my father.

The Dark Days

This was the beginning of the dark days, the dark days that dragged on for years.

I stayed in Petrozavodsk—at least there my mother knew I was safe and warm—and Mother, Paul and Aino huddled together in the house in Uhtua and waited for word from Father.

But no word came.

Without Father's income, money was tight. For awhile, Mother continued working at the orphanage, and Paul and Aino met her there every day after school to get a hot meal—often their only meal of the day. But then the orphanage director was arrested and Paul and Aino were no longer welcome. Then Mother lost her job. There was so much fear, everywhere.

Oscar Corgan had been arrested, and people were terrified to have anything to do with the rest of the Corgan family, fearing our misfortune might rub off on them. All the families of arrested men were treated this way; guilt by association had already resulted in dozens of arrests.

December came, with howling winds and heavy snows, and on one of the coldest days Mother was evicted from the little house she loved on the banks of the river. There were no rooms available in town, and as the wife of an "enemy of the people," Mother knew the authorities would not welcome her there in any case. All the families of "enemies of the people" were being chased from their quarters. Some ended up living in barns or saunas.

My family moved into an abandoned house on the outskirts of Uhtua—a tiny broken-down peasant house with shattered windows and no heat. But Mother said she was grateful to find even that. They lived on eighty rubles a month that she earned sewing pillowcases. Mother grew thin; most of her rations she gave to Paul, who was in a growing spurt and was constantly hungry, or to Aino, who was small for her age, and sickly.

I was lucky. The principal of my school took pity on me and arranged for a stipend so that I could continue my education. It was a risky thing in those days, for a native Russian to befriend an immigrant—especially an immigrant whose father had been branded "an enemy of the people." But Anna Stepanovna Lyagina was a strong-minded woman, who had a clear sense of justice, and was afraid of nothing. I was eternally grateful for her assistance. She even offered to let me move into her quarters, but I refused. I didn't want to cause her more trouble. She had already risked so much for me.

Instead, I moved out of the Hotel and into the quarters of my good friend Edith Lehtinen. Every month, I received a voucher for thirty rubles, which I immediately turned over to Edith's parents, Toivo and Hilda, to pay my room and board. Despite my despair, this was a lively place to live. Toivo Lehtinen was a tailor. He worked in one half of the room, and the family lived in the other. Hilda had strung up a curtain dividing the room in two. Thanks to Edith's kindness and the kindness of her parents, I wasn't deprived of a sense of home.

Oscar and Katri Corgan pose for their wedding picture.
Hancock, Michigan, 1914

The Corgan children: Paul-1, Mayme-3 and Leo-9
Superior, Wisconsin, 1926

Pioneer Camp at Workers' Park in Ishpeming, Michigan, 1930.
Photo courtesy of Eugene and Dorothy Järvi

Amateur actors at the Finnish Tower Hall, Superior, Wisconsin, 1920
Katri Corgan is at the left.

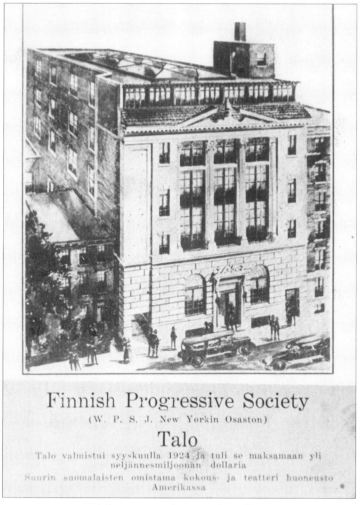

Finnish Progressive Society

(W. P. S. J. New Yorkin Osaston)

Talo

Talo valmistui syyskuulla 1924 ja tuli se maksamaan yli
neljännesmiljoonan dollaria

Suurin suomalaisten omistama kokous- ja teatteri huoneusto
Amerikassa

The New York Finnish Hall,
completed in 1924 at a cost of a quarter million dollars

The Corgan family passport photo:
Aino, Mayme, Katri, Paul and Oscar
New York City, 1934

Petrozavodsk in the 1920's

Clothes were scrubbed and washed in Petrozavodsk homes, then were rinsed
in the Lososinka River—a pleasant task on a summer day
but bitterly cold work during the long winters.

The Penikka Panti (Puppy Band) at the head of
the First of May demonstration in Petrozavodsk, 1934.

The Välibarracks in Petrozavodsk, eight houses in all,
were constructed in 1931-32 by Finnish-Americans.

Oscar Corgan
Superior, Wisconsin, 1910

Karjalais-Suomalainen Sosialistinen Neuvostotasavalta
Карело-Финская Советская Социалистическая Республика

KUOLINTODISTUS
СВИДЕТЕЛЬСТВО О СМЕРТИ

ЦЮ № 084835

Kansalainen
Гр. *Корган*

(sukunimi — фамилия)

Оскар-Фредерик Карлович

(nimi ja isännimi — имя и отчество)

on kuollut (*18/VII - 1940*) *восемнадцатого июля*
умер(ла)

(vuosi, kuukausi ja päivä kirjoitettuna ja numeroilla)

тысяча девятьсот сорокового года

(прописью и цифрами год, месяц и число)

kuoleman syynä on ollut *рак желудка*
причина смерти

josta siviiliasian kuolinrekisteriin
о чем в книге записей актов гражданского состояния о смерти

1956 vuonna *ноября* kuun *21* päivänä
года месяца числа

on tehty vastaava merkintä
произведена соответствующая запись за № *53*

Kuolinpaikka: Karjalais-Suomalaisen SNT:n *?* kaupunki
Место смерти: Карело-Финская ССР, город

piiri kylä
район селение

Rekisteröintipaikka *с. Ухта районное бюро*
Место регистрации

(siviilirekisteritoimiston nimi ja paikka —

ЗАГС

наименование и местонахождение бюро ЗАГС)

Annettua *ноября* v. 19 *56* г.
Дата выдачи

Siviilirekisteritoimiston johtaja
Заведующий бюро записей актов
гражданского состояния *Карилло*

Финский (Карельский) кз. Гознак. 1947.

Oscar Corgan's death certificate, issued November 30, 1956
It records the date of death as July 18, 1940, the cause of death
as stomach cancer and the place of death as unknown.

СВИДЕТЕЛЬСТВО О СМЕРТИ
KUOLINTODISTUS

Гражданин (ка)
Kansalainen *Корган*

Оскар-Фредерик *Карлович*
имя, отчество — etu- ja isännimi

умер(ла) *9. 01. 1938 года   Девятого января*
on kuollut   число, месяц, год — päivä, kuukausi, vuosi

Одна тысяча девятсот тридцать
(цифрами и прописью — numeroilla ja kirjoittamalla)

восьмого года

в возрасте *51* лет, о чем в книге регистрации актов о смерти
vuoden ikäisenä, mistä siviilirekisterin kuolinluetteloon

19 *56* года   *ноября*   месяца *21* числа
vuoden   kuun   päivänä

произведена запись за № *53*
on tehty merkintö n:o

Причина смерти   *Расстрелян*
Kuoleman aiheutti

Место смерти: город, селение
Kuolinpaikka: kaupunki, kylä   *Не установлено*
район
piiri
область, край
alue, aluepiiri
республика
tasavalta
Место регистрации   *Райотдел Калевальского*
Rekisteröimispaikka   наименование и местонахождение органа ЗАГСа —
siviilirekisteritoimiston nimi ja sijaintipaikka

" *16* " *августа*   19 *91* г.
v.

Заведующий отделом (бюро)
актов гражданского состояния
siviilirekisteriosaston (toimiston)
johtaja   *Хейнонен*

ГИ   № 390096

М Ѓ Гознака. 1988. Финский (карельский) яз.

Oscar Corgan's second death certificate, issued August 16, 1991.
It records the date of death as January 9, 1938, the cause of death
as "shot" and the place of death as unknown.

Mayme and Milton Sevander
Petrozavodsk, 1965

Commemorating Oscar Corgan's 100th birthday, October 2, 1987

Seated at center front: Andy (Leo's son)

Row 1(left to right): Bertha (Paul's wife) with grandson Paul, brother Paul with grandaughter Liza, Mayme, sister Aino, daughter Stella's son Philip

Row 2 (seated): Natasha (Leo's wife) and daughter Katrina; kneeling: Leo; standing: Igor (Stella's husband), Stella, Anna (Paul's daughter) with husband Igor, Paul's son Andrei holding Zhenya, Anna's son and Kristina, Alexei's daughter, Alexei (Paul's son) with newborn Anna, Lyudmila (Alexei's wife)

In 1991, Mayme Sevander stands at the Duluth, Minnesota, Civic Center
(site of the cover photo) waving an American flag
Photo courtesy of Joey McLeister

Early every morning Toivo's partner, Moses Sormunen, came by to work. He would burst into the room, stomping snow from his feet and blowing on his fingers to warm them, his cheeks and nose rosy from the cold. Hilda would offer him a cup of tea, and after he had warmed up, he would join Toivo on the other side of the curtain. There they would sit, cross-legged on the floor, stitching garments all day long, talking and laughing. Moses was an elderly bachelor who had come from California, and sometimes he would sing as he stitched. Listening to them sing and crack jokes and tell stories kept me sane, I think. During the months I lived there, the room became an island of reassurance in a terrifying, depressing world.

All that year, I buried myself in my studies. I took no joy in learning, but it kept my mind off the thousands of questions I had about my father. I knew that my mother was making inquiries, but I also knew that she had been warned not to ask too many questions or else she, too, might be taken away. And then what would happen to Paul and Aino?

Paul wrote and told me that most of his friends were in the same situation he was: fatherless, penniless, nearly hopeless. So many Finns had been arrested. Years later we found out that these mass arrests and imprisonments were happening to different ethnic groups all over the country, but where we were, the focus was on the Finns and Karelians.

We didn't know it then, of course, but these sweeping purges had begun with Sergei Kirov's assassination at the end of 1934. There had been purges before that, when Josef Stalin came to power in the 1920s, but they were mostly political purges, party purges, Stalin getting rid of people who opposed him or could do him harm.

We had heard nothing about those purges, either, at the time that they were taking place. Stalin controlled the press, he controlled everything. Everything we knew, we knew because he wanted us to. We believed he was a good man, a staunch Communist, a worthy successor to Lenin. We did not know, until many years later, that he was behind the purges. We did not know that he was methodically killing us all.

But that is what was happening. Most of the Finns were not just being arrested. They were being imprisoned, tortured and then shot. Their bodies weren't returned to their loved ones; they had no proper funerals or respectful final resting place. Instead, they were dumped by the hundreds into mass graves in the wilderness, and dirt was bulldozed on top of them. At home, their families waited for years, often in vain, for word of their fate.

It is now widely believed that Stalin secretly planned the assassination of his friend, Kirov—and then, feigning outrage over the murder, used the incident to spark a new wave of purges. But this time, it wasn't just party members and rival politicians being killed. This time, Stalin tried to wipe out every vestige of criticism, nationalism, opposition or independence. These purges affected every citizen across this whole enormous country.

"Purge" isn't a big enough word to describe what took place in those years; it sounds too clean, too sanitary. This was more than a purge; it was a slaughter, a holocaust. Stalin killed the peasants, the farmers, the people of the land. Without farmers to grow the food, famine swept the country, and thousands more died, slowly starving to death.

He killed people of other nationalities and backgrounds and languages. He killed indiscriminately and unconscionably. He killed hundreds, then thousands, then tens of thousands, then hundreds of thousands. After the dust settled and the purges ended and Stalin was finally dead, we found that our great leader, our trusted "Uncle Joe," had killed twenty million of his own people.

And among those that he killed were hundreds of American Finns who had sailed to his country as invited guests, as experts and laborers who wanted to help socialism succeed.

The fear. How can I describe that fear? Russians' lives have been ruled by fear since the days of Ivan the Terrible. As adopted Russians, we American Finns adopted that fear.

In Petrozavodsk, the earnest struggle to build a socialist society was over. Instead, my schoolmates and I lived in a constant state of terror. We didn't know who was friend and who was foe. When I found out that one of our good Finnish neighbors had helped take away my father, my faith was shattered. Finns were no longer sticking together; no one was sticking together. We all looked out for ourselves and our own families; it was suicide to trust further than that.

Often, the people who were arrested were tortured and their families threatened. They were questioned relentlessly: "Who recruited you to work against the government? Who are your cohorts? Tell us or we'll arrest your wife, your son." And under torture and fear, even innocent people would sometimes break and blurt out someone's name. And then the NKVD (the secret police, later called the KGB) would show up on that person's doorstep and take them away, and the questioning would start again.

We were afraid to confide in anyone. We were afraid to speak. We were almost afraid to think. Every day, we would hear of another arrest, and if it was somebody we knew, we couldn't help but think, "I wonder what he is saying about me?" We were ashamed to think that, ashamed to let that thought cross our minds when our friends' fathers or brothers had been arrested and were in such danger. But we couldn't help it. How could we trust, when so many had been taken?

Nights were the worst. I lay awake and imagined I heard the sound of boots trudging down the empty street toward a door, heavy boots that would ensure the doom of another person and the devastation of another family. The men usually came in threes—troikas, they were called—and they almost always came at night.

It was hard for me to sleep. It was hard for everyone to sleep, those days. Friends told me how they went to bed each night with their bags packed, just in case. Other friends disappeared and showed up again weeks later, frostbitten and thin. We had thought they'd been arrested, but they had been hiding among the islands of Lake Onega or in the Karelian forest.

We didn't know what was behind this. We still had faith in Stalin. We believed that he had no knowledge of these arrests and that if he did he would surely stop them.

Some people tried to escape the country. My family did not. It was unthinkable for us to leave without knowing the fate of our father, and in our hearts we believed that things would improve, that these years of terror would end and we could pick up where we had left off.

There was no opportunity to leave, in any case. It was impossible to get word to relatives in Finland, Sweden or the United States about what was going on. The mail, if it got through at all, was heavily censored. Without a foreign passport, we could not travel, and the men who had taken my father had taken all of my family's papers—passports, birth certificates, marriage license, everything. Uhtua was close to the Finnish border, tantalizingly close to my mother's childhood home, but the border area was closely guarded. Men with guns patrolled the crossing points, and according to rumors, they didn't hesitate to shoot.

It was clear that the Finns who had been invited to the Soviet Union to help improve the country had somehow, suddenly become hated intruders. We were forbidden to leave. Our adopted country had become a terrifying prison. In Uhtua, restrictions against Finns grew tighter. The Finnish-language paper was shut down. Speaking Finnish in public was banned. Suddenly, all the schools became Russian-language schools and the Finnish-speaking teachers were thrown out of work. People dared speak Finnish only in whispers, in their own rooms, behind closed doors and around only the most trusted of friends. The rest of the time people like my mother, who knew no other language, stayed silent, worried that the wrong words would slip out and then they, too, would be taken away.

These were such desperate times. The arrests were all we talked about, but in whispers, always in whispers, and then we felt a knot in our stomachs, a fear that someone would hear us, that a hand would fall on our shoulder and a voice would say, "Come with me," and that would be the end of us. But we couldn't help ourselves; we had to talk; stories went around despite the risk.

Did you hear about Mr. Hillukka, the one-armed Finnish bachelor from Canada? He drowned himself in Lake Onega to avoid arrest.

We had our heroes, too, people who had been tipped off that the troika was coming and who had gotten away. That was the amazing thing about the troikas: If you managed to elude them, they rarely came back a second time. What did the arrests mean? The randomness made it that much more chilling.

William Jukkala, who had come over from Hancock, was one who fled to the forest when he heard the troika was on its way. He was there ten days and was forced home again by cold and hunger, but the troika never came back to his house.

Walter Maki, a pianist from Canada, heard that the troika was coming for him. He hid under an overturned boat for three long days. How did he eat? Why didn't he freeze to death? My friends and I didn't know the details, but we did know that he managed to escape the purge.

It was certain death to get caught defying the NKVD, but still there were those who dared. We heard the stories of courage and escape and passed them on.

We rejoiced at the news of a Mr. Zarubin, a Russian man we had never met. He warned a group of Finnish loggers in the nearby lumber camp of Matrosa that NKVD agents were waiting to arrest them all when they came to get their pay. That day, none of the loggers showed up to collect his salary. And, at least for that one day, none was arrested.

Every now and then, someone would see a glimmer of hope. Someone would hear from a relative in prison, and we would all rejoice, knowing, at least, that the man was still alive. My friend, the actor Orvo Bjorinen, got a letter from his father, who had been taken away months before. It was just a brief letter, postmarked from Komsomolsk, so far away—near Vladivostok, on the other side of the country. Orvo was ecstatic to get the letter. It asked for cigarettes, and Orvo's mother ran out and bought cigarettes and sent them off to Komsomolsk.

But the tobacco came back, weeks later, the package marked "No such person." And the Bjorinens were once again filled with despair.

My own despair never lifted. We got no letter from Father, no request for tobacco, no sign at all that he was still alive. Without Russian-language skills, my mother was limited as to where she could write for information, and she was afraid to raise a fuss.

The young Karelian woman who used to visit Father to discuss politics, Paraskeva Vasilyevena Lobskaya, wrote an impassioned letter to the NKVD on his behalf. I was terrified for her safety and deeply grateful at the same time. Sending such a letter was risky and I didn't want anything to happen to her. But her letter, eloquent and sensible, seemed wonderful to me. When they read this, they must see they have the wrong man, I thought. She tells them quite clearly that my father was a loyal Communist and a tireless party worker.

Weeks went by, and we waited for the reply, but when it came I was crushed with disappointment. It was a form letter, stating curtly that the NKVD does not make mistakes. Chillingly, the writer of the letter used almost the same words poor Kalle Sevander had used: "We do not arrest innocent people," it said.

When I saw that letter I knew I had reached the breaking point, and I recklessly sent two of my own, demanding news of my father and insisting that he be set free. I sent one letter to the NKVD and one to the Supreme Soviet. And then I waited.

The replies came on the same day, and they both asked me to come to their headquarters for a personal interview.

At the NKVD office on Karl Marx Street, I was told that my father had received a ten-year sentence. Ten years! I mulled it over as I walked to my second appointment at the military tribunal in Lenin Square. In ten years I would be twenty-five, my father would be sixty-one. The year would be 1948. Everything would have changed so much. But at least he would finally be home.

But at the military tribunal, I was told that my father had been given a fifteen-year sentence. The NKVD had told me he was in prison in the Soviet Far East, near Vladivostok. The military official told me that he was in the Kazakh Republic in the South.

Lies. It was clear they were telling me lies. I blew up at the military agent. "Where is he?" I demanded, clutching his desk top with both hands. "You tell me one thing, the NKVD tells me another! You say fifteen years, they say ten! You say the south, they say they east! Where is my father? Where is he?"

The agent leaned over his desk and sneered at me. "You'd better watch yourself," he said in chilling tones. "You're just like your father. If you were of age, we'd put you in the same place he is."

I was a few months shy of my fifteenth birthday, and his threat meant nothing to me. The only emotion I felt was pride: I was proud to be compared to my father. And I vowed to go on with my search.

Enemy of the People

I looked up from my mother's garden where Aino and I were pulling weeds. The white-hot August sun blazed down on our backs as we worked, and though the sky was an intense, cloudless blue, I hoped that rain would come soon. The little tomato and potato plants were precious to us, but they were already drooping. I was afraid that if the heat wave continued, we would have nothing to eat all winter.

Aino wore a little red-and-white kerchief to keep the sun off her head, but she still looked miserably hot. I worried about her. She was eleven now, but she looked much younger. She had always been frail, and in the last few years she had grown thinner and weaker. Her eyes looked huge in her peaked face. Ever since our first winter in Petrozavodsk, when she had fallen ill with dysentery, her health had been fragile. She had spent several weeks in the hospital then, and the doctors had told my parents there was no hope she would recover. She had surprised them and lived, but she was never very strong after that. She tired easily, and she never grew plump and red-cheeked, like the other Finnish children.

I wished we could feed her better—lots of rich, creamy milk and eggs might have made a difference—but we just couldn't give her enough good things to eat in Uhtua. Provisions in the stores were scarce, and what there was was rationed.

I had been in Uhtua for most of the summer, since school had let out in June. But this summer was different from the one before. This time, I had to get special permission from authorities in Petrozavodsk to travel, since Uhtua was near the Finnish border. No one was allowed to travel freely in border areas—especially not families of "enemies of the people."

And when I finally arrived, instead of bringing me back to the cozy house that I remembered so fondly, Mother, Paul and Aino met me at the bus station and took me to their new home—a ramshackle Karelian cottage on the outskirts of town, even more cramped and cold than our old room at the Hotel in Petrozavodsk.

No longer did laughing Finnish children gather along the banks of the river to swim and sunbathe. This summer, it was hard to find anyone who was laughing. The Finn Hall was closed, and there were no more "white night" dances. The Midsummer Festival had been canceled. All sense of freedom and joy was gone.

It was an eerie feeling, walking down the streets of Uhtua and seeing almost no men. There were women, plenty of Karelian and Finnish women, with head scarves over their blonde hair and worried looks on their broad faces, and there were lots of children. But there were almost no men. Over the course of the winter and spring, most of the families had been shattered. Like mine, their fathers had been arrested and taken away, their wives and children left to make their way alone.

By now, my own father had been gone for eight months. And in all that time, there had been no word.

The discrimination against the Finns intensified. Paul's request to attend Artek, the famous Young Pioneers Summer Camp in the Crimea, had been turned down. His school had recommended him, which was a great honor, and Mother had allowed herself to hope that he would be accepted. At the camp, Paul would have lived a carefree life for three months and been fed three square meals a day. But the officials said that the son of an "enemy of the people" wasn't welcome with the Young Pioneers.

Instead, Paul began working on the collective farm outside of town. I think he was just as happy driving a team of horses there as he would have been at the Pioneer camp, but Mother felt the sting of rejection. "An enemy of the people," she said, shaking her head as she feather-stitched the hem of one of the beautiful pillowcases she sold. "How can they say that? How can they believe that?" And she surreptitiously wiped away a tear, quickly, so that we would not notice and lose heart. But we noticed. How can you not notice when your mother is crying?

The money Paul earned helped keep us together that summer. He took care of the horses and drove loads of logs and hay from the woods and fields back to town. He was only thirteen years old, but he thrived on the work, growing strong and tan. The farm provided him with a noon dinner each day and paid him a small salary as well, which our family sorely needed. When he got his first paycheck, he stopped at the bakery in town and bought a loaf of white bread and a whole jar of jam. We celebrated that night. It was the first white bread any of us had had in months; we always ate the Russian brown bread because it was cheaper and more filling.

After working in the garden for several hours, I looked over at Aino. She was wilting in the summer heat, her face pale and tired. "You've done enough weeding," I said. "Why don't you run down to the river and have a swim? It would cool you off."

But she just shook her head. "I'd rather stay here," she said. We never discussed it, but since Father's disappearance no one in the family felt comfortable being separated from the others, even for a short time.

A tall man wearing a hat turned up the walkway of our house.

I shaded my eyes with a hand to see who he was, but he was nobody I knew. He came right up to me, though, and asked for my mother by name. "She's inside," I said, standing up and brushing the dirt from my knees. Aino and I followed him into the house.

My mother was sitting by the window, stitching a pillowcase. She sewed pillowcases endlessly, hoping to produce enough of them to earn more than her salary of eighty rubles a month, but her hands were stiff from arthritis and I knew that every stitch was painful. The man handed her a card, which was printed in Russian. She shook her head and gave it to me to read.

"The truck will be around tomorrow," the man said, and left.

"What did he say? What did he want?" my mother asked in Finnish. She was grasping the pillowcase in her hand, the white cotton bunched between her fingers, the needle dangling, forgotten, from a long white thread.

I read the card through twice to make sure there was no mistake, and then I looked at her. "They are sending us away," I said, trying to keep my voice steady. "We have twenty-four hours to pack up and leave Uhtua. They are sending us to Kem. A truck will come around tomorrow to take us there."

My mother did not cry. She was too tired, too beaten by all the events of the last year to cry. She just nodded slowly. "Kem," she said. "They are sending us into exile."

I put my arm around Aino and we stood there, three women, together but alone.

The truck came the next afternoon, a big, drab, green military truck, with a canvas top over its open back. We had to share the space with our neighbors, the family of Juho Luoma, a Finnish-Canadian who had been arrested shortly after Father. His wife and three children were also being sent to Kem.

It was clear that one truck could not hold all the household goods of two families. We packed only the essentials—warm clothes, cooking utensils, blankets, the folding table, the day bed, my mother's heavy black sewing machine—and left everything else behind. "We'll be back," my mother said, trying to sound brave, but her eyes filled with tears when she saw me standing in the doorway, a book in each hand but no room left to pack them.

"Remember this? *Gems of the World's Best Classics*," I said, rubbing my thumb along the soft leather of the book's binding. "This was the book that was going to help me get into college. Remember? You and Father brought it all the way over here from Superior."

"We'll be back," my mother said again, her voice firmer this time. "The book will be here when we get back. And don't worry about college, Mayme. You're going to college. There's no question about that."

But I lacked the faith of my Mother. After her back was turned, I slipped the two books—*Gems of the World's Best Classics* and a fine, leatherbound Webster's English dictionary—into one of our boxes. I wasn't going to take the chance of losing these reminders of America—and of my father—forever.

We were not the only families to be sent into exile that day. All the families of the arrested men were taken. Our truck was one of thirty that were filled with furniture, kettles and frightened children, and together we made quite a sight. One after another, the drab, green trucks rumbled through the streets of Uhtua and out to the countryside along the bumpy road, up hills and down, through potholes and dust. For 182 kilometers, the convoy jolted along at high speed, and we clung to each other and to the sides of the truck for dear life. When the trucks slowed and bunched together, we breathed the oily exhaust. When the trucks spread out, our driver sped up, flinging us from side to side in the back of the open truck as he accelerated around curves.

Our destination was not Kem. We stopped there only briefly and then continued on out of town. The road was just two deep ruts in the dirt with scraggly fireweed and buttercups all around and the huge, tall pines of the Karelian forest pressing in close.

"We are going to the end of nowhere," my mother said with a

sigh. She had wrapped one arm around Aino and was holding onto one of our boxes with the other. She swayed back and forth with the movements of the truck, and her face looked tired. There were grimy streaks of dust along her nose and cheek.

The family of Juho Luoma didn't speak to us at all. His wife and children clung to their possessions and stared out at the passing forest. They were friends of ours—good, friendly people—but this day they looked beaten. We didn't talk to them, either. What was there to say?

The wind whipped my hair, the truck exhaust stung my eyes, and I fought the urge to cry. I wondered if we would ever see Father again, ever see Uhtua again. I wondered how Father would find us when he got out of prison—if he got out of prison. I wondered if our lives would ever return to normal.

When the convoy finally stopped, it did, truly, seem as if we had reached the end of nowhere. We were at Latushka, a primitive logging settlement carved out of dense forest on the rocky banks of the Kem River. The trucks jolted to a halt, and we stood up, stiff and sweaty and dirty, to look around.

There was not much to see—a few rough-hewn wooden buildings, some horse carts, a couple of outdoor privies, and a dirt path that looked as if it led to nowhere. Clusters of ragged children gathered in doorways and watched us indifferently.

My mother tried to hide her discouragement. "Let's unpack," she said briskly. "And then we can have some dinner. I could use a cup of tea, couldn't you, children?"

But when we walked into the log building to which we all were assigned, our spirits fell. It was worse than the Hotel; it was worse than the ramshackle house in Uhtua. Here, we were in a huge, open barracks with sixty other families. The barracks was divided in two by a common wall, and each half was assigned to more than seventy people—children, men and women. A big stove stood at one end for cooking and heat, leaving the other end of the room cold and drafty. Little Aino's eyes grew huge and round as she looked around the room at all the strangers we would be living with for who knew how long. And who knew why? She grabbed my mother's hand and held on tightly.

All across Karelia, families of Finns, families of the men and women who had been arrested, were being swept up from towns and settlements and dumped into exile, sent to live in wooden barracks, like this one, in the rocky, barren wilderness. We didn't know why. There was no one to ask. There was no time or opportunity even to find out who to ask. Summer was winding down, and after the brief, colorful autumn was over, we knew there would be another bitter winter. There was much that we must do before then.

At first, I think, we viewed one another with suspicion. It was hard to reconcile ourselves to living in one room with so many strangers. But gradually, we began to develop a sense of camaraderie. This was more than us Finns against the NKVD; it was also us against the forces of nature.

In northern Karelia, winter digs in early and hangs on long, and we knew that we would not all survive the winter in housing like this. The wooden building was uninsulated and had only drafty, single-pane windows, and we knew it was going to be difficult to keep the room warm once the cold set in. We banded together and did what we could to weatherproof the barracks. We stockpiled logs for fuel and assigned families with the smallest children to the warmest part of the room.

My family staked out a space in the barracks for ourselves and strung up blankets for privacy. But there was no way to shut out the sounds of the other people, talking, coughing, snoring, belching. Or the smells—the smells of unwashed clothes and unwashed bodies, the cooking smells of cabbage and potatoes.

Paul was given a new job. No longer looking after a team of horses on a collective farm, he was now driving a tractor and debarking logs in the logging camp. It was terribly hard work for someone only thirteen years old, but Paul knew he was the man of the family now, and he didn't complain.

My job was to count logs. Although I was only fifteen, hour after hour I stood on a rickety, floating platform in the bay of the Kem River, a chart in my hand, making notes. The platform was square with a large hole in the middle, like a doughnut, and its gray boards were wet and slick. It bobbed ceaselessly on the waves, making me glad I wasn't prone to seasickness. All day long I sat there and waited for logs to drift past. The men who sent the timber down the river called out the category of each log as it floated by: "Firewood!" they would yell, or "Paper wood!" And I would make an X in the appropriate space on the chart. It was a tedious job, a boring job, and, as autumn set in, an increasingly cold and uncomfortable job. Day after day, hour after hour, I sat on the bobbing platform, shivering in the cold and the fine, gray rain, making hatch marks and trying to stay warm—and, as often as not, trying to stay awake.

I wasn't getting much rest. I was still worried about my father, and thoughts of him crowded my head at night, chasing away sleep. Night after night I found myself lying, tense, in my blankets, staring at the ceiling and listening to the sounds of people all around me: wailing babies; snoring old men; invisible, restless people on the other side of the curtain who moved about in their own small space, also unable to sleep.

Mother had a job, as well, taking in washing to supplement the small hoard of money she had saved from selling Father's gold watch. She hadn't wanted to sell the watch—she had hoped to keep it and give it back to him when he returned—but times in Uhtua had grown so bad that finally she'd had no choice. Food was available, though not in great variety, but prices were low, so she was able to stretch the money quite economically. We lived for a long time on the proceeds of that watch and the little she earned scrubbing other people's laundry on a washboard. Her hands, once slender, beautiful and capable, were now red and cracked, the knuckles painfully swollen from arthritis. It hurt me to even look at them.

November came, with its bitter winds and leaden skies and the terrible, grim anniversary of Father's arrest.

On the afternoon of November 5, a storm blew in. The sky was heavy and gray, and a strong wind set my platform to bobbing more vigorously than usual. I slid from side to side rhythmically as I waited for the logs to float past, but the river was beginning to ice over, and work was slow that day. I yawned and shivered in the wet, chilly wind and then yawned again. I was still so tired, and as the minutes ticked by with no logs to count, I felt my eyelids drooping. I played tricks on myself to stay awake: I bit my thumb; I clenched my fists, digging my nails into my palm; I stretched. I thought of getting to my feet and jumping up and down, but that seemed like too much trouble. I yawned again. And then I was in the water.

The shock of the icy river water woke me. My woolen clothes became soaked and heavy and began to drag me down. Instinctively, I grabbed for the planks of the platform and screamed. Some of the loggers dropped what they were doing and ran to pull me out. They bundled me in blankets, tossed me in the motorboat and zipped me back across the bay to the barracks.

My mother looked terrified when they brought me home, dripping wet and wrapped in blankets, but I was only cold, not sick. She put me to bed and brewed me a cup of tea and sat by my side the rest of the afternoon, telling me stories of her girlhood in Finland and her early days in America. Gradually, the warmth returned to my toes and fingers, and my teeth stopped chattering.

The barracks seemed almost cozy in the late afternoon, with our curtain drawn for privacy, most of the people out working and my mother sitting by my side. *We can do this,* I thought. *We can survive exile like we've survived everything else. We'll be fine until Father comes home.*

But a few weeks later, typhoid struck our camp.

It swept through the barracks, and in a matter of days, dozens of people were tossing and moaning on their cots. The smell of illness was everywhere. The typhoid was caused by our inhumane living arrangement. Cleanliness was impossible in a place with no running water, a place where so many people lived and cooked and slept in such close quarters. Many people also suffered from lice, and some of the lice carried disease.

There were no ambulances in Latushka. As people fell ill, they were loaded up on horse wagons and carted the seven kilometers into Kem, where a small wooden hospital building faced a snow-covered graveyard.

As people all around us became sick, we prayed that Aino stay healthy. She was one of the frailest of the children, and we knew that if she became sick, it was unlikely she would survive. Aino did stay healthy. And Paul and Mother stayed healthy. In my family, only I fell ill.

One afternoon, on one of our rare days off, I went with a group of other teenagers from Latushka to see a movie in Kem. Movies had been one of my favorite forms of entertainment back in New York, where I sometimes spent an entire Saturday in the theater, watching newsreels and cartoons and two feature films. But here, movies were a rare and cherished treat.

We walked into Kem along the snowy railroad tracks, lifting our knees high to get through the drifts. We arrived at the theater just a few moments before the film began, paid our kopecks and found our seats.

As the lights went down, I began to feel uncomfortably warm, but I put it out of my mind. Who wouldn't feel warm, I reasoned, after trudging seven kilometers through deep snowdrifts and then squeezing into a small, crowded theater? I'm not sure what happened next, exactly—my companions said I merely toppled over in a dead faint. I regained consciousness in the arms of my friends, who carried me the whole long way back to Latushka.

My mother, faced with having me carried home twice in two

months, put me to bed again, but this time it was clear that I was terribly ill. A few hours later, they bundled me up and put me into the horse cart that had already carried so many other people to the hospital in Kem. I thrashed about, trying to throw off the blankets, telling my mother I was too hot. She kept pulling the blankets around me and saying, "Mayme, Mayme, it's December. You must stay warm!" But I tossed and moaned and shivered and tried to pull off the blankets again.

They put me in the hospital's pre-death ward. There was no hope, the doctors told my mother bluntly, but they would try to make me comfortable. They cut off my hair close to the scalp and wrapped me in icy sheets to bring down my temperature. But the fever still raged, and for days I was on the brink of death.

One morning, after days of feverish babbling, I sat up when the nurse walked in the room. "My father was here last night," I told her, no hint of delirium in my voice. "My father came here to see me, and he brought me some grapes." She looked alarmed. She didn't know that my father had been arrested, but she also had never known my father to visit me.

"Grapes?" she asked. "Where are they?" Grapes were unheard of in that part of the Soviet Union, especially in winter.

"They're over in that drawer," I said. I felt calm, and happy now that I had finally heard from my father. The nurse pulled open the drawer, but of course it was empty. I sank back into my pillows, devastated. I had been so sure I had seen my father, so sure he had come to visit me.

After that, my fever raged even higher.

I was in the hospital for three months. Outside my window I could see the white crosses in the graveyard across the way. In my more lucid moments I vowed that I would not end up there, not yet. And I didn't. Slowly the fever abated, and I began to recover. When I got home—thin, pale, head shorn, shaky—I found that thirty-three other people in our barracks had fallen ill. Fifteen of them had died.

The authorities panicked at this wave of illness, and they began making arrangements to give us better living quarters. Some of the families were moved out of the barracks and into small cabins that had once housed loggers. My mother was one who was given a private place to live, but by now she had had enough of exile. Families were permitted to leave now, as long as they didn't return to Uhtua or any other town in the border area.

"We can't stay here," she told me one morning shortly after I returned home. "You almost died, Mayme, and Paul is working himself to death in that lumber camp. We're not staying here much longer." She reached over and touched my head, where my shorn hair was starting to grow in, spiky and blonde. "Poor Mayme," she said. "You look like a porcupine."

"I was hoping it would grow in curly," I said, trying to make her laugh, and she did, a shaky laugh that trailed off in a sigh. "This place has brought us nothing but sorrow," she said. "As soon as we can arrange it, we're leaving."

A Grave Injustice

All over Soviet Karelia, Finns—both American Finns and Finnish Finns—had been sent into exile. We later heard of many of our friends from Petrozavodsk who had been sent to work at other logging camps or to islands in Lake Onega. No one place was better than another. Everywhere people were sent, they suffered. Families lived wherever they could find shelter—in barracks or abandoned houses, even in old saunas and outbuildings.

One group was sent to Kalajoki Island in Lake Onega, where they worked as loggers and lived in an old prison barracks. Most of them had never handled a saw before, but the government demanded they become loggers, so loggers they became.

Others were sent to nearby Lime Island, a rocky, barren place where the women and children found shelter in old stables and worked all day, mining lime. A few dared to escape by stowing away on the lime boats. Of those who stayed, scores died of starvation and malnutrition. One woman, Bertha Lahdeskorpi, lost both her children on Lime Island; one died of hunger, the other died instantly after eating a pebble of deadly lime.

Some people defied exile, though it made no difference in the end. A friend wrote me in Latushka, telling the story of Katri Lammi, a Petrozavodsk opera singer. "The truck came to take her away to Lime Island," my friend wrote. "She stood on the back, holding onto its sides and surrounded by pots and pans and a few broken chairs, singing the Soviet anthem. It made quite a picture, this old green military truck driving off down the road in a cloud of dust, and Katri Lammi standing in the back, singing at the top of her lungs:

> Boundless is my Motherland beloved.
> Thousands are the rivers, lakes and woods.
> There's no other land you'd ever covet.
> Here you breathe as freely as you should.

It gave the song a whole new meaning, let me tell you."

All that spring, I worked at an eating house for the workers in Latushka, and my family made plans to leave. There were no guards or barbed wire keeping us there; we simply were forbidden to return to Uhtua or anywhere else in the border area. Before we could leave, I had to apply for my passport. It was 1939, and I would pass my sixteenth birthday in July. In the Soviet Union, that was the age of majority; every citizen had to apply for an internal passport at age sixteen.

So one afternoon I went into Kem and filled out the application. I was promptly turned down. I had no birth certificate or identification papers—they had all been confiscated when my father was taken—and the authorities told me they couldn't issue a Soviet passport without seeing the proper documents.

"Go back to America," they told me. "Or go to your father's homeland, Sweden. We can't help you here."

My mother agreed with them. "Go, Mayme," she said. "Get a foreign passport and go to Sweden. Oscar's relatives will take you in. We'll join you there just as soon as we can, I promise."

But I wasn't about to flee the country and leave my family

behind. Despite her urging, I knew that my mother needed me. And I wanted to be here when my father was released from prison.

I didn't know it then, but the decision to stay may have saved me. Years later, Lempi Tolonen, a Canadian Finn, told me her story. When she turned sixteen, she applied for a Canadian passport. Her father, David, had already been arrested as an "enemy of the people," and her mother, Hilda, urged her to flee to Canada. But Lempi's request for a Canadian passport was denied. Several years later, Lempi was arrested and charged with having attempted to go abroad. Though she was several months pregnant, she was thrown into prison, where she gave birth to her daughter.

I didn't know the dangers at the time; I just felt that I couldn't leave the country without knowing the fate of my father. So early one morning, I boarded the train for Petrozavodsk, prepared to battle the higher authorities for a passport.

I returned to Latushka a day later, tired and discouraged. The Petrozavodsk official also had refused to give me a passport. Without one, I couldn't work or travel or be issued housing. My mother and I decided the only thing I could do was try again.

A few weeks later, I boarded the train once more for the long trip to Petrozavodsk. I was prepared to argue with the NKVD all day long, if I had to, and maybe all night long, as well.

But when I arrived, I found there had been a change of personnel. The new official was a friendly man with a kind face. He wore a gray uniform and a cap with a red star. In a rush of words, I told him my problem, and he smiled and picked up the telephone. He called the Kem official directly and barked at him through the phone, giving me a conspiratorial wink as he spoke. I imagined, with some pleasure, the man in Kem cowering on the other end of the line.

The conversation was brief. "Don't worry, young lady," the official said as he hung up the phone. "When you get back to Kem, your passport will be waiting for you, along with an official apology for the delay."

I started to stammer out my thanks, but he interrupted me. "Also waiting for you will be some money to reimburse you for these trips," he said. "You shouldn't have had to come here at all, let alone twice." And he escorted me to the door and tipped his cap in farewell.

I had dinner that night with my old principal, Anna Stepanovna, and told her of my victory. "That's wonderful, Mayme," she said, filling my teacup. "But when your family leaves Latushka, where will you go? Are you coming back here?"

"We haven't decided," I said. "My mother's sister, my Aunt Maria, is living in Pai. Her husband was arrested after my father was, and I think my mother would like to be near her."

"But Pai is just a little lumber camp," Anna Stepanovna said, frowning. "They don't even have a school there yet. You need to get on with your education. You've missed a whole year already."

"I know. I want to get back to school," I said. "But I have to go where I can live."

"You can live here, in Petrozavodsk," she said. "You can type, can't you? I seem to recall your saying you had some experience with office work. Well, we need a secretary and a librarian at the school. It would pay you 350 rubles a month. It's a day job, but you could go to school at night."

My eyes widened at the prospect. "I'll have to talk it over with my mother," I said. "I'm sure she'll agree. I'll let you know as soon as I get back to Kem."

"It would be a lot of work," Anna Stepanovna went on. I barely listened. A lot of work! I'd done nothing but work hard for the last two years, counting logs, scrubbing dishes, clearing tables. What a joy it would be to work in a clean, warm office and spend my evenings with my books.

How much I owe Anna Stepanovna! She had rescued me once after my father was arrested, arranging for the stipend that allowed me to continue my schooling. Here she was, rescuing me again, offering me a job and a chance to further myself. She owed me nothing. She was Russian, not Finn, and she had a great deal to lose. But she put herself out on a limb for me. I don't know why. Maybe she saw potential in me, or maybe she was trying to atone for the injustices of Stalin's regime. Maybe she simply believed that young people represented the future of the Soviet Union and needed to be helped and nurtured along the way. Whatever her reasons, she was a true hero, one who took risks and invested in others. All the way back to Kem, I daydreamed on the train, thinking about how hard I would work at my job and my studies, if only I were given the chance.

My mother saw the wisdom of the plan immediately. Once again, the family would have to split up, but she knew how important it was that I get on with my schooling.

That August, just before school began, Paul and I took the train to Pai to arrange the move, and officials there issued my family a small, but clean, room. Aunt Maria was delighted at the news. She had heard nothing from her husband, Antti, since his arrest, and she was heartened at the thought of being around family.

And then, alone, I boarded the train for Petrozavodsk. I would be staying with an old school friend, Ruth Merila, whose family had come to Karelia from Grand Rapids, Michigan. Ruth was living with her mother, Helen, in one room not far from the school. It was a large room, and they had space for me because her sister, Florence, had taken a teaching position outside of town. And her father, Leonard, had disappeared. He had not been seen since his arrest two years before. It was the same sad story, tragic no matter how many times we heard it. The troika had come in the night, taking away Leonard Merila—a good Finn, a good father, a good Communist—and leaving his broken family behind.

I lived with the Merilas all that year. They gave me one corner of their room, and I stashed my possessions out of the way—my few clothes, my winter coat, my copy of *Gems of the World's Best Classics* that was my inspiration. I was gone so much I hardly saw the Merilas at all. I worked all day, dashed back to the room for dinner and then hurried off to my classes. I studied whenever I could—late at night while Ruth and Helen slept, in the early morning over breakfast, during my lunch break at noon. I didn't get much sleep that year, but I did graduate from the eighth grade.

Petrozavodsk had changed during our year in exile. The city had grown, and it was busier, with more cars and many more people. Military men swaggered up and down the boardwalks, handsome young Karelian, Russian and Finnish men in snappy uniforms. One by one, young men we had attended concerts with or ice skated with or sat next to in class were called up to serve. We didn't understand why such a large military was needed, but when the war with Finland broke out in November 1939, we were glad to be well-defended.

We were all shocked to read in *Pravda,* the Communist party newspaper, about how little Finland had attacked the Soviet Union. Brave Soviet soldiers—thousands of them ethnic Finns themselves—dashed across the border to fight, and in many cases to die, in the Winter War.

It was a bloody war. Our school was turned into a makeshift hospital to accommodate the casualties, and four times that winter I arrived at school in the evening only to be told that there were so many casualties that classes had been moved to another building in another part of town. The winter nights were unbelievably cold that year, the temperature dipping to sixty and seventy degrees below zero Fahrenheit and staying there for days and nights at a time. The glittering white snow squeaked beneath our feet and lighted our path as we trudged from the school to the temporary classroom across town. We had no cars, and the buses ran only sporadically. The cold filtered through our thin felt boots and ran up our legs. Our breath was cold in our lungs, our nostril hairs froze and our scarves stuck to our faces with frost. But skipping classes was unthinkable.

Having our school turned into a hospital made the war real, but the losses made it even more so. Some of our young comrades who went off to war, young and handsome in their uniforms, were brought back, shot up and bloody, to die in the school-turned-hospital.

We didn't understand the truth behind the Winter War, but we found it hard to believe that Finland would attack the powerful Soviet Union. It wasn't until nearly fifty years later that it became clear to the Soviet people that Finland had not started the war. The Winter War was begun by Stalin, who had wanted to take from Finland a corridor of land near Leningrad. The Finns resisted courageously, donning white clothes to camouflage themselves in the snow and hitching sleds of ammunition to reindeer. Silently, they glided into the forest on cross-country skis and blew up the Soviet tanks. The Soviet casualties were great, but the Finns were outnumbered and could not hang on forever. When the war ended in March 1940, the Soviet Union had lost an incredible 200,000 men, but Finland had lost the war. The border was changed.

I heard from my mother and Paul regularly. Aino suffered from one cold after another but seemed to be holding her own, they wrote. Paul worked all that winter clearing lumber roads. In the fall of 1940 a school opened in Pai, and he started seventh grade.

There was no word from my father.

I worked for the school district that whole school year. In the summer of 1940 I found a new job working for the government. I was a secretary to the executive council of the Zareka district of the city. The pay wasn't any better, but my hard work earned me the bonus of a sturdy pair of shoes—no small thing, in those days. The executive committee was housed in the left wing of a building on Ulitsa Uritskovo. The District party and the Komsomol committees were housed in the right wing. The Komsomol—also known as the Young Communist League—was the youth organization of the Communist party. Its district secretary was a charming, friendly woman named Tatyana Samoznayeva. We chatted often in the hallways, and she knew about the tragedy that had befallen my family. Her husband was the general secretary of the Komsomol, and as warm and approachable as his wife. His name was Yuri Andropov, and forty years later, he would become the leader of the Soviet Union.

It was while I was working for the executive committee that I decided to apply for membership in the Komsomol. I had spent my childhood as a Young Pioneer, and I had been brought up in the spirit of communism. Despite the unhappiness that had overtaken our country, I still believed firmly that the Communist party would prevail and turn things around. My application was approved by the executive committee's Komsomol unit. But when it was sent on to the district committee, my membership request was denied.

I was crushed. In those days, almost all the young people joined the Komsomol. Those who didn't were outsiders, with no say over how things were run in their schools or places of work. I was never one to be comfortable sitting back and taking orders; I wanted a say in my life. And without membership in the Komsomol, this would be very difficult.

The committee gave no reason for my rejection, but it was clear to me that the injustice done to my father was still reverberating through our lives.

Then, a few weeks later, a friend once again stepped in to help. Tatyana Samoznayeva returned from vacation and spotted my Komsomol application on someone's desk with the word DENIED stamped in red across it. "What is the meaning of this?" she demanded. "Why has Mayme's application been denied?" When they explained, she argued with them heatedly. "It's not her father who is applying, it's Mayme," she told them. "She has been commended for her work and has proven herself to be a loyal Soviet citizen. This application must be reconsidered. This is a grave injustice."

My application was resubmitted to the next district council meeting, and this time my Komsomol membership was finally approved.

During all this time, I was still attending school at night. It wasn't an easy life, working all day and attending class four nights a week, but it was a life that many people at that time were leading. Most of us—especially us American Finns—weren't going to let anything stop us from completing those classes and getting that diploma.

My family never gave up looking for Father. One clear morning in May 1941, when I arrived at my job at the District Soviet, I was met by the committee chairman, Ivan Mikhailovich Antokhin. His face was ashen and he was holding a piece of paper in one hand. He didn't greet me, just thrust the paper at me and demanded, "Mayme, what have you done?"

"What are you talking about?" I asked.

"This is a subpoena from the NKVD for you," he said. He was trembling. "It's for today—this morning at ten!"

"They've answered!" I said, snatching the paper from him in relief. "I wrote them about my father," I told him, tucking the subpoena into my book. "I went right to the top, this time. I wrote the chairman of the NKVD."

I hadn't told anyone—not even my mother—not wanting to endanger anyone else.

"But what about yourself?" Ivan Mikhailovich asked. "Aren't you afraid you've gotten yourself into trouble?"

"I need to know the truth," I said. "I need to know what happened to my father." But though my words were brave, inside I was quaking. For nearly four years now, everyone had been living in fear of the NKVD. Few people were ever called to the Gray House, as the NKVD headquarters on Komsomolskaya Street was called. And it was common knowledge that not everyone who walked in that front door walked back out again.

At half past nine, Ivan Mikhailovich had a car brought around to take me to my appointment. I told him I could easily walk there, but he insisted. He shook my hand cordially, and some of the women I worked with hugged me. No one said it, but it was clear that none of them expected to see me again. I was scared to death inside, but I hoped that I would finally know the truth.

The driver let me out in front of the Gray House—a big, forbidding building with barred windows and a huge front door. On the left side was a small window where people sought permission to enter. I walked up to the window and presented my subpoena and documents.

"Wait here," said the man inside, and vanished.

He was gone a long time. I stood on the street, watching the people pass by in their light spring clothes, staring at the puffy clouds in the clean blue sky. It was not quite summer, and I was struck by the beauty of the morning. It had rained the night before, and large puddles glinted in the street, reflecting the sky. The slender trees that lined the side streets had put out baby leaves, light green in the chilly sunlight. I waited, and while I waited I wondered if this would be the last time I would see this street, the last time I would see a morning.

The man came back. "This way," he said. I began to follow him through the front door. As I crossed the threshold, I paused for an instant. I hadn't realized how nervous I was, but my foot was trembling so that I could barely step.

I followed him up a broad staircase to the second floor, hardly daring to look around. I saw long hallways with wooden doors and heard the muffled metallic clacking of typewriters. We came to a closed door on the second floor. He motioned for me to open the door and enter. Then he disappeared.

The doorknob felt very big in my hand, and very cold. I turned it and pushed open the door. The room was large. My feet sank into thick carpeting as I walked across to where a man was sitting behind a desk, a big window behind him and a comfortable chair before him. He motioned for me to sit down.

"You must be Mayme Corgan," he said, rising to greet me. He was tall and broad-shouldered, dressed in a military uniform. His face was rugged and severe, but his eyes were kind. "My name is Mikhail Ivanovich Baskakov. I have read your letter."

He paused, but I didn't say anything. He knew what it was I wanted to know. There was no point in my asking again. And besides, if I stayed quiet, he wouldn't see how my teeth were chattering.

"Your letter touched me deeply," he said, sitting down again and looking at me with sympathy. He sounded sincere. "I have received many letters from people like you, people who are looking for their loved ones. I don't have the time to answer them all. But your letter—it sounded so sad, so filled with despair. It sounded as though your life were over."

I forgot my fear and leaned toward him earnestly. "I must find out where my father is," I said. "You must tell me how I can write to him. You must tell me how long he will be gone. He's been gone for more than three years now, without a word."

Mikhail Ivanovich leaned back in his swivel chair and gazed out the window. I tried not to think of my mother, squashed into one bare room with Paul and Aino, while this man sat alone in an office big enough to house three families. He turned back. "Who helped you write that letter?" he asked suddenly.

"No one," I said. "I'm sure you can tell by the mistakes that I did it myself. I've only been studying Russian for a few years, and my grammar isn't perfect."

He seemed to relax after that. "I know you love your father," he said. "I know you believe in his innocence. And I admit, some mistakes have been made. There's no doubt about it. But you must get on with your life. You're young. Your future is ahead of you. How old are you now? And how are you living?"

I told him that I was not quite eighteen and had a job working for the district council. "Well, you see?" he said. "That's quite a start for someone as young as you. Keep at it and work hard, and I'm sure the day will come when you will be a deputy yourself."

This was a new thought for me. I had been under the impression that families of "enemies of the people" would be denied any kind of future under the current Soviet system.

Mikhail Ivanovich picked up the phone and asked another official to come into the room. "This young woman is missing some property," he said when the man arrived. "Some items were confiscated when her father was arrested, and she would like them returned. Take down the information and see what you can do to locate her possessions."

For the next ten minutes, I described the typewriter, the family photos, the camera, the radio, the notebooks and all the other items that the NKVD men had taken the night of my father's arrest.

"We cannot promise that we will find your belongings," Nikolai Ivanovich said as I prepared to leave. "But we will do what we can. And we will certainly let you know if we hear news of your father."

It was with great excitement that I wrote to my mother that evening, telling her that we might soon have our possessions returned and—much more important—find out Father's where-abouts. In my mind, I clung with hope to the words of Nikolai Ivanovich: "I admit, some mistakes have been made." That could mean anything—anything. It could mean that they had made a mistake in arresting my father. It could mean that my father would be coming home.

Trusted to Serve

Stalin had taken most of the radios. We got our news from *Pravda,* the Communist party newspaper, and from loudspeakers attached to the outside of apartment buildings. June 22, 1941, was a Sunday. I had gotten up early, planning to spend the day at the Dynamo, a recreation center on Lake Onega. It was the beginning of summer, and my friends and I planned to rent a boat and go swimming. But the news we heard early that morning changed everything. The words blaring from the loudspeakers were scratchy with static, but the message was chillingly clear. The Nazis had invaded the Soviet Union. We were at war with Germany.

Everyone was astounded. Although the Soviet Union had been involved in the beginning of World War II, when our troops paved the way for the German invasion of Poland, Stalin and Hitler had signed a peace agreement, and we all had been certain that the pact would keep us safe from Hitler's greed for territory. Instead, Hitler had violated that agreement. His Luftwaffe had launched a dawn bombing attack on the Soviet Air Force that morning, destroying most of our air power. German troops were now streaming across the border toward Leningrad, Riga and Minsk.

From that morning on, our lives were devoted to the war effort. According to the government news reports, we had nothing to fear. The Red Army was one of the best equipped in the world. We would turn back the fascists in no time. The loudspeakers told us that every day.

But for the present, the Germans were making tremendous strides toward Leningrad, and the Finnish soldiers, who had joined the Nazis, began to march toward Petrozavodsk.

Every day, I heard the latest war news before anyone else. Just a few weeks before, I had gotten a new job as typist at the Tass news bureau. It was an exciting place to work, with the news crackling across the radios all afternoon, and I hoped to stay with Tass for some time to come. I was making a little more money now, enough to afford a room of my own, and my mother came from Pai to live with me. Paul and Aino planned to join us when school let out.

My mother had aged over the winter: there were deep circles under her eyes and her thick brown hair was streaked with gray. Every few days, she asked me the same question: "Is there any news of your father?"

There never was. I remembered with remorse the hopeful tone of the letter I had written her just a few months before. Now that war had broken out, I knew the officials would have no more time to spend on our cause. Finally, at orders from Nikolai Ivanovich, an NKVD official called me and told me that. I related his message to Mother. "With the war on, they're too busy to continue to search for our property," I told her.

"But what of the search for Oscar?" my mother said. "I can understand why the property isn't of importance now, but what of a man's life?"

I didn't know what to tell her. "He said they have heard nothing new," I said. "I have to believe him."

Everyone in Petrozavodsk spent the summer of 1941 digging

trenches and planting spiked stakes to deter the advancing Finnish troops. We made explosives, we pasted paper over the windows, we saved soap shavings and collected scrap metal. For a time, we each forgot our individual worries and sorrow. We were all working together to protect our country.

The recruiting stations were open twenty-four hours a day. More and more men were called up to serve, and as the male editors at Tass were drafted, I was given more responsibility. "Genius" Niskanen, who had served in the Winter War, was called up again. Again, he was sent to the front. His sister, Ruth, was conscripted into the army as well, leaving her mother and little brother behind. Milton Sevander, the handsome young trombone player I had begun to keep company with, was called up. The town began to empty out.

In September, the order came for many of the Karelian towns to evacuate. With the Nazis closing in from the south and the Finns advancing from the west, it was clear that Petrozavodsk was in danger of falling. Aino was alone at Pai when the evacuation card arrived. She tidied up the room, packed a few necessary belongings, and boarded the crowded train for Petrozavodsk. The room, she told Mother and me when she arrived, was left as though she had just gone to work. The cups were on the table, the broom was behind the door.

Paul took the train to Petrozavodsk the next day, and we all went down to meet him. I had never seen the train station so crowded. Evacuees from the settlements filled the station and spilled out onto the concrete platform, pushing past one another and dragging bundles of all shapes and sizes behind them. Some had steamer trunks and suitcases; others had their clothes tied up in broken cardboard boxes. A few had brought livestock with them: goats, and a handful of chickens. There was no panic, but a sense of urgency permeated the crowd.

The Nazis had already cut off the railroad to Leningrad. The only way south was by water: by barge across Lake Onega, and then down the Volga River. By now I had been promoted to an editor at Tass. I loved my job and I told my family I wanted to stay behind.

"You can't stay here, Mayme!" my mother said, clutching my arm. "The enemy will be here before you know it!" It made no difference anymore that my mother was Finnish herself; the Finns had thrown their lot in with the Nazis, and now they truly were our enemy.

"The government is evacuating, too," I told her. "Everyone is going to Medvezhegorsk. The deputies, the committee chairmen, everyone. Tass is going, too, and they need me. I would like to go with them." Medvezhegorsk was a small city about 150 kilometers straight north of Petrozavodsk.

"We'll worry about you, Mayme," my mother said, releasing my arm. "But don't you worry about us. There are three of us. We'll stick together and do just fine."

That night I helped them pack. My mother had filled the steamer trunk with food and clothes, and I found room for extra socks and woolens of my own. She had also brought her best dress along—a lovely blue silk dress that she had stitched with her own hands. "You keep this," she told me. "I want you to have it." I protested, but she shook her head. "There's no use my taking this into evacuation," she said. "Where would I wear it? It wouldn't even do to keep me warm. I always meant for you to have this dress, anyway. You might as well take it now."

I took the dress, but I knew I would never wear it. It belonged to my mother, and I would save it for her to wear again when the war was over.

On the morning of September 17, 1941, I said goodbye to my family. Mother, Paul and Aino, clutching their bundles of food and clothing, were packed onto a barge with scores of other evacuees. The barge rode low in the water, burdened with people and possessions. Two tugboats waited to pull it across the lake.

The autumn sky was clear, and the birch trees had already turned a bright gold.

My mother's huge brown eyes were melancholy; they had never regained the spark they had lost the winter Father was taken. When she spoke, her voice was brave and calm. "Take care, Mayme," she said. "Let us know how you're doing." We didn't know exactly where they were headed—perhaps somewhere on the other side of the Ural Mountains, far to the east—but we promised that somehow we would write, and when the war was over, somehow we would find each other again.

The tugboats started their engines, and slowly the heavy barge began moving through the water, away from Petrozavodsk, and—we all hoped—away from danger. I stood on the lake shore and watched it go. Then I headed back up Karl Marx Street toward the deserted city center.

We took the train to Medvezhegorsk—more than a hundred of us, all government workers—but we stayed there only a month. The Finnish army was advancing steadily into Karelia, and in November we had to evacuate again. This time we headed for Bielomorsk, a tiny town even further north, on the south shore of the White Sea.

In Bielomorsk I worked at night, taking in the news and supplying it to the local newspapers for the next morning's edition. I sat at a typewriter, with a radio to each side, and typed the stories and articles as quickly as they were broadcast. The static was terrible. I developed a knack for listening through it, but I often went home in the early morning hours with my ears ringing from the strain.

My job was interesting, though exacting. I had heard stories of people who had been severely punished for making mistakes, and that gave me extra incentive not to make any myself. One unfortunate editor was arrested, or so the story went, for leaving out the "r" in "Leningrad." Without the "r," the word takes on a whole new meaning—it means "Lenin the reptile"—and the man was charged with insulting the founder of our country.

There was not much to do in Bielomorsk, other than work. Every evening I listened intently as the war news crackled in, and as I typed, I wondered about my family. Several weeks after we left Petrozavodsk I heard reports that two barges filled with evacuees on Lake Onega had been bombed from the air by the Nazis. Hundreds of lives had been lost—all innocent people, trying to escape the terrors of war. My heart ached for those poor people, but I was deeply thankful that my family was not among them. And, of course, I wondered constantly about my father. The evacuation worried me. What if Father were released from prison, only to find that we had all left Petrozavodsk? While it didn't seem likely that he would be released during the height of war, I thought how terrible it would be if he were to come home to a vacant house. What could he think, but that we had abandoned him?

One morning early in 1942, I was summoned to the office of Yuri Vladimirovich Andropov. One of his duties was recruiting young Soviets for reconnaissance missions. When he sent for me, I was honored.

Because I was Finnish, he told me, he wanted me to go behind enemy lines and do reconnaissance for the Red Army. My blonde hair and Finnish-language skills would allow me to move around in Finland, and my intelligence and wits would keep me alive.

I was thrilled at the idea of being a scout against the Nazis. What a wonderful opportunity to serve my country, to outwit the enemy and to experience a great adventure, all at the same time. I was only eighteen—young enough to be swept away by the romantic aspect of it all, without worrying too much about the danger. But I felt compelled to be honest. "My father has been arrested, you know, as an 'enemy of the people,' " I reminded him. But of course he already knew that.

We talked for a long time. Yuri Andropov chose his words

carefully. I do not remember exactly what he said, but his implication was clear. My father was innocent, he all but told me. He assured me that one day my father's honor would be restored, and that until then I should not have to worry that I would continue to suffer for that tragic mistake. He told me that they trusted me to serve my country. They trusted me to be a scout.

Weeks went by, and I heard nothing more. I had almost put being a scout out of my mind when I was called to the Komsomol Central Committee again. Yuri Andropov summoned me into his office. This time, he told me that my training would begin immediately. My supervisor at Tass had already been ordered to release me from my duties there.

All that spring and summer, I trained with the military in Bielomorsk. I was not alone. Many Finnish Americans had agreed to serve as reconnaissance scouts. For nine months I studied photography, radio communication and topography. I learned to take apart radios and reassemble them. I studied the international Q-code. I learned to read maps, take pictures and develop film. All this time, I kept waiting for them to begin language lessons. My Finnish was adequate for me to get by in Petrozavodsk, but I was nowhere close to being fluent. I knew the minute I opened my mouth around a native-born Finn it would be clear that I was a foreigner.

I had found out where my family was, and I wrote Mother regularly. Mother's letters were brave, but I could read between the lines. It was clear that she and Aino weren't getting enough to eat, and the situation sounded desperate. My ration cards provided me with adequate food, and housing was free, so every month I slipped a money order for most of my salary into an envelope for Mother. I wanted to send her more—I wanted to send her food and clothing, as well—but wartime regulations were strict. It was forbidden to bog down the mail service by sending packages. I kept asking, though, and finally, because I was a soldier, I was granted special permission to send her one package.

I did my best to make that package memorable. I found the biggest box I could and packed it with everything I could think of: all my warmest clothes, mittens, socks, underwear. I knew that survival in evacuation depended on two things: staying warm and getting enough to eat. The wartime economy had sent food prices skyrocketing, so I loaded that box with things for them to sell: trinkets, spoons, scarves. On an impulse, I added my mother's blue silk dress, figuring she could sell it for a good price in the Urals. I could always get her a new silk dress when the war was over.

It was still forbidden to send food through the mail. During the war, people lived on what they could get with their ration cards, and everything was very closely watched. But my family was on the verge of starvation, and I wasn't going to sit by and do nothing. I went to Major Matveyev, one of the officers in Bielomorsk, and asked for his help.

Together, we set off for the army post office, where my package was examined and approved. And then, as I was getting ready to seal the carton, the major began to flirt with the postal clerk. She was a stout, scowling woman, and at first she looked at him with suspicion. But he kept flattering her, winking at her, telling her that her hair was beautiful and asking her where she had gotten such dimples. She began to giggle and blush at his attention, and as he distracted her, I began to empty my pockets into the carton. Tins of meat, lumps of sugar, pieces of candy, packages of tea—all the nonperishable food I had been able to save from my allotment over the last few months went into that box. And when my pockets were empty, I sealed up the package and sent it off.

It was a miracle that the package got through. Aino said later that Mother burst into tears when she saw all those clothes, all that food, and money, besides. "What has Mayme done?" Mother sobbed. "Has she robbed a bank?" But they took the money I had sent and went off to the bakery. Before the war, one thousand rubles would have bought thousands of loaves of bread, more bread than Mother and Aino could have eaten in a lifetime. But this was wartime, and food was scarce. With my thousand rubles, Mother bought two loaves of bread—two loaves of bread, at five hundred rubles apiece. That's all.

My military training continued into the fall, though I didn't know exactly what it was I was training for. The military was quite secretive, and all I knew was that a partner and I would have to jump out of an airplane into Finnish territory. I didn't know what my orders would be after that, and it was hard for me to think beyond the jumping part, anyway. I had never been in a plane, let alone jumped out of one, and while my adventurous side was attracted to the idea, my practical side was apprehensive.

When the time came for my one and only practice jump, I was elated. Four of us, all young women no older than seventeen or eighteen, boarded the Douglas aircraft at a small airfield outside of Bielomorsk. In the interest of security, the military made sure we were all strangers to one another. I'd never seen those women before, and I wasn't even told their first names.

As the plane took off, I felt, at first, as though I'd left my stomach behind. But as we soared above the treetops, my nerves settled down, and I realized how much I was enjoying myself. We could see for miles. The road was just a thin dirt path from up there, and off to one side, far in the distance, I could see the glinting surface of the White Sea.

We knew what to do. We had received plenty of instructions on when and how to pull the rip cord, and how to land, and what to expect, but we were all afraid. Below us, everything looked soft and hazy, the treetops like green cotton balls, but we knew quite well how hard the ground was. And none of us wanted to go first.

In the end, they pushed us out. The plane dipped and soared above a large field, and one by one we tumbled out, pulled our rip cords, and hoped for the best.

For an instant, I was alone in the world, weightless, floating to earth like a dandelion seed, surrounded by nothing but blue sky. And then I hit the ground with a thump and fell over. I stood up and brushed off my knees. I was shaky but smiling, and so were the other three women. Though we all begged for another practice jump, it was clear we didn't need it. We were ready to go. It was time for our mission.

We were split into groups of two, a man and a woman in each group. Ever cautious, the military insisted that our partners be strangers to us. They had matched me with a young Finnish-American man, but after a little checking it became clear that I knew him far too well for their comfort. It was Milton Sevander, my sweetheart from Petrozavodsk. So the officers found me another partner.

In January 1943, I was summoned to the headquarters to meet him. While waiting in the major's office, I heard a familiar voice out in the hall. "Listen!" I said. "That's Kalervo Koski!" The major scowled. Kalervo was to be my new partner.

I had known Kalervo for years. He had come to Karelia from Massachusetts with his family. It was too late to find me a third partner, and I doubt if the attempt would have been successful anyway. We American Finns were a close-knit group, and it would have been almost impossible for them to find a Finn I didn't already know.

Kalervo and I were sent from Bielomorsk to Tcherepovetsk, on the Leningrad front. We arrived after midnight on a bitterly cold January night. Our mission was still unknown to us, though we knew we had to fly out the next day. After a few hours of sleep, we were summoned to the headquarters, where three unfamiliar officers waited. First Kalervo, then I, went in to be questioned.

"Are you ready to be dispatched?" I was asked. I was relieved at the question; now was the time to let them know our training hadn't been sufficient. "No," I said (Kalervo later told me he said the same). "Our radio and map training have been excellent, but we've had no language instruction. We need Finnish-language training if you want us to pass as natives."

The middle officer's face contorted into a snarl. "Coward!" he snapped, leaning toward me. "You are afraid to go! You would rather be sent to a labor camp?"

I didn't know what a labor camp was, but I knew I didn't want to go there. I didn't want to go anywhere. I wanted to do my part to help rout the Nazis. "No, sir," I said. "There are other things I could do to help the cause. I could be a radio operator at the front, or a messenger. It's just that my language skills aren't good enough yet for me to be a scout. My accent would give me away for sure."

"There's another place for people like you to go," he said. "You are not trusted to go into action." I was hustled out of the room.

Within a few hours, Kalervo and I found ourselves at the Tcherepovetsk train station, bewildered and frightened. We were on our way to UVSR-232, near the town of Vologda. We were on our way to a Soviet labor camp.

Too Late for Mother

We walked for miles along the deserted road that led to the labor camp. The frozen snow crunched beneath our boots and the midnight sky above us glowed with a cold, full moon. Barren fields lined the road on either side. Neither Kalervo nor I would admit we were afraid. We tried to boost each other's spirits, but we were both apprehensive about what lay ahead.

I couldn't understand why the military would take us—two strong, intelligent people willing to risk our lives for the war effort—and lock us up. How could we be considered cowards when we had gone through months of military training, jumped out of an airplane and made it clear we were not just willing but eager to fight the Nazis? But in those days the Soviet Union was run by fear and ignorance. The officials didn't care whether our concerns about our lack of language training were valid, and they found it easier to punish us than to investigate.

By the time we reached the labor camp, my toes had no feeling in them, and my fingers were numb and white. At first glance, the camp seemed to be nothing more than just a handful of rough buildings. Then I noticed the dozens of smoking stovepipes that were sticking out of mounds in the frozen ground. These, I found out later, were the dugouts where the prisoners were forced to live. The whole place looked desolate and forbidding, cold and silent in the snow, but in a way, I was glad we had finally arrived. Whatever it was we were going to encounter there—imprisonment, discipline, forced labor—I was ready to face it. I preferred to know my fate quickly rather than delay it for days or hours.

We walked into the first building we came to, blinking in the bright light and stamping the snow from our boots. A cheerful-looking officer came out from around the desk to greet us. His name was Jim Sinaiski, and he told us he was a Ukrainian from Canada. He ushered us into the room almost as though we were guests, rather than inmates, telling us how pleased he was to meet two people he could converse with in English. "I won't even ask you anything yet," he said. "I know you're tired and half-frozen." And he gave us each a steaming bowl of soup and brought us to a dugout to get some rest.

On our way outside, Jim gave us a few words of advice for the night. "Put your knapsacks under your head," he warned. "Leave your sheepskins on. Kalervo, don't let anyone know you're with a girl. Mayme, leave your hat on, cover as much of your face with it as you can. And as soon as you wake up, rush back to the headquarters. We'll decide what to do with you in the morning."

The next day, Jim got in touch with the camp commander's wife and told her about me. He didn't think it appropriate or safe for a young woman to stay in the dugouts with all the men, and Ludmila Mikhailovna agreed. A Finnish girl named Emma Huitar had shown up at the camp a few days before and was staying in a corner of someone's room. Jim and Ludmila Mikhailovna found a tiny room in one of the houses where camp employees and officers lived, and Emma and I moved in there.

Most of the prisoners at the labor camp shared the same "crime": We were ethnic minorities—Estonians, Latvians, Jews, Poles,

Romanians and Finns. Like Kalervo and me, many of the Finns were reconnaissance scouts, a few of whom had returned from missions only to be incarcerated.

Kalervo was sent to work on a construction site with the other men, but Emma and I were allowed to stay indoors, typing, filing and cleaning. As labor camps go, ours was not as bad as others I heard about later, after the war. We had no guard houses, no ravenous watchdogs, no barbed wire. The food was adequate, and we even had a small amount of freedom. During our spare time, we were allowed to walk to Vologda, the nearest town. Vologda was a typical small Russian town of a few churches, a scattering of old-fashioned buildings and unpaved streets. But there was one remarkable thing about the town: It had a library. That library became my haven; it saved me from complete despair. Over the long months of my imprisonment, I made friends with some of the other prisoners, did my typing and filing, and, every chance I got, walked into town to spend a few hours reading in peace.

There was not much else to do. We prisoners formed a Komsomol group which met now and again, and sometimes we even put on musicals and dances. But no matter how we tried to be cheerful and optimistic, the fact remained that we were still prisoners. I wrote to my family, to friends in Bielomorsk and to friends in the army, but I had no way of knowing if my letters got through. I heard from no one. It was as though I had dropped off the face of the earth.

Every few months, we were questioned. Military officials from headquarters or other bases would show up at all hours to ask us the same questions, again and again. It was frustrating and point-less, but we were in no position to complain. We were, after all, prisoners, though we'd been accused of nothing more than cow-ardice and had never been on trial.

One morning in November 1943, I was summoned to the office. A new officer was there, inquiring after a "girl in a brown sheepskin coat." When I came forward, he immediately began yelling at me. It took me a few baffled moments before I recognized him: He was the snarling officer from Tcherepovetsk who had banished Kalervo and me to the labor camp nearly a year before.

"Why didn't you tell me you were an American?" he demanded. "We aren't fighting Americans! We're fighting Finns! The Americans are our allies!" He thrust a paper at me. "Take this to the military commissariat in Vologda. They'll give you a ticket back to Bielomorsk." And he turned to go.

I was amazed, but I couldn't let him leave so quickly. "Wait!" I said. "What about the man I came here with—Kalervo Koski? He's American-born, too. He's from Massachusetts."

"Kalervo Koski is a man," the officer said. "That's different. He'll have to stay until the war is over."

Nothing I could say would change his mind.

At the military commissariat in Vologda, I begged and wheedled and finally won a compromise. Kalervo Koski would have to stay, but they did agree to grant freedom to Emma Huitar as well as to me. She and I were issued white cards to present to the military commissariats in our own towns, and then we were free to go. It was late November when we set off—I for Bielomorsk, and Emma for Kandalaksha, further north, where her parents lived. We had been in the labor camp for a little less than a year.

The white cards indicated that we were invalid for active service in the military, but I never turned mine in. I figured I would hang onto it, just in case I needed it in the future. No one ever asked for it.

In Bielomorsk, I picked up my life where I had left it nearly two years before. I returned to Tass, where I was given a warm welcome by my colleagues. Within a few days I was back at work, typing and transcribing and taking dictation from war correspondents all night long. One of the first people to welcome me back was Yuri Andropov. I ran into him one afternoon when I was on my way to my office. The snow was deep, and I was carefully following the narrow foot path when I looked up to see him in front of me. He embraced me in a warm hug. "I'm happy to see you're alive and in good health," he said. "It's unfortunate, the things that happen in war. But it's all behind you now. Welcome home."

"Thank you," I said. "I'm glad to be back."

The war dragged on, but by 1944 Finland had had enough, and they sought a peace agreement with the Soviet Union. The Finnish army began to pull out of Karelia, and it was decreed safe for people to return. Immediately, I sent an invitation to my family, urging them to return. In March, I received a telegram from my mother. She and Aino were leaving evacuation and heading for Bielomorsk. I had no idea where Paul was; he had somehow been separated from them during the war.

The trains were overloaded those days, with thousands of people on the move, returning from evacuation and trying to get home. Aino told me later that she and Mother bribed a railroad official to get space on a cargo car that was going as far as Moscow. They sent me another cable from Moscow, but there was no way of predicting when they might finally arrive. As it turned out, they were stranded for several days, afraid to leave the Moscow station lest they miss a train, until they finally found space on a crowded train bound for Bielomorsk.

The trains were running on no schedule at all because military cargo had top priority. I returned to the railway station again and again, inquiring about their arrival, until finally the agent told me that a trainload of evacuees was on its way. After I heard that, I refused to leave. I waited for hours on the platform. I tried to read, but I could not concentrate. It had been three years since I had seen my mother and sister, and now each minute that ticked by felt like another year.

Finally, in mid-afternoon, the train pulled in, chugging black smoke and screeching its brakes, and crowds of people began spilling out its doors. They were stick figures, all of them, thin and bony, with shadows under their eyes and rags on their backs. I was horrified, imagining what deprivations these people had had to endure. I walked up and down the platform, searching anxiously for my family. The ragtag crowd began to thin out, and I began to lose hope. Then I heard my name.

"Mayme." A girl stood before me, bone-thin, with deep circles under her eyes. I had walked past her a moment before, not recognizing her. It was Aino. She had left Petrozavodsk as an elfin-faced child. Now she was seventeen years old, with enough experience behind her for a lifetime. Beside her stood an elderly woman, thin and gaunt. She wore mended clothes, and on her feet were shoes woven from tree bark. "Mother?" I whispered, and the woman looked up. Then I knew her; I would know those sad brown eyes anywhere.

We embraced, but I held my mother gingerly. She looked so thin and weak I was afraid of crushing her in my arms.

I took them back to my room and gave Aino a ration coupon and some money. She went out and came back with powdered milk—the first milk that they had had in weeks. Mother had worked as a dairymaid during the evacuation, but she had been told not to drink the milk because it was for the soldiers. And even though she had worked unsupervised at night, and even though she was wasting away from lack of nourishment, she was too honest to steal. She milked the cows, she carried the brimming pails, but she drank no milk. And month by month, she had grown thinner and weaker. Now, she sat next to me on my bed, and I held her hand. Her skin was so thin it was almost transparent. "I'm so glad you're here, Mother," I said. "Don't worry, we're going to fatten you up." But she was so frail I doubted my own words. It seemed impossible that a person could be so thin and still be alive.

Because Aino had passed her sixteenth birthday, she needed a passport. She had no documents, so the officials weighed her, guessed her age, and assigned her a new birthday: February 28. She was amused by the Soviet bureaucracy—her real birthday was Valentine's Day, February 14—but she complied with all of the paperwork and was issued a passport. Shortly after, she began working in a sawmill outside of town. Mother was too weak and ill to work, but the government wouldn't issue her a ration card if she were unemployed. Without a ration card, she would receive no food. So she took a job cleaning houses, and Aino and I did the work for her. Even then, Mother refused to rest. She used the extra time to take in laundry. "I know, I know," she said, whenever we scolded her. "But I can't sit still during the day, girls. I'm just not used to it. And laundry isn't that difficult."

But she looked so tired all the time.

Sometimes in the afternoons we would sit and talk, and it was during those long hours that we shared our war experiences. They told me that the last they had heard of Paul he was in a hospital in Tchelyabinsk. I went out immediately and sent him the same official invitation to return to Karelia that I had sent Mother and Aino. But we heard nothing from him.

I told Mother and Aino about my experiences in the labor camp, and they told me about what had happened to them during the evacuation. We had communicated by letter, of course, but so much more can be said face to face. The hardships they had endured and the horrors they had seen were etched forever on my mother's creased face.

They started their story at the beginning, at the barge trip across Lake Onega.

By the time the barge got to the Volga River, Mother said, evacuees had already begun dying. From time to time the tugboats would pull the barge over to the river's edge, and the dead would be hoisted onto land and buried. Paul, being young and strong, helped dig graves. He grew accustomed to lifting dead babies and dead young women and dead old men, settling them into holes in the ground and shoveling dirt over them. It never became easy work, but it became familiar.

Everyone grew dirty and thin. The weather was cold and

blustery. Food was scarce. Blankets were damp. People who had thought to bring samovars were the luckiest, because they could boil water. The others had no way to cook, no way to heat anything. The barge grew less crowded.

In November, after two months on the barge, the refugees were brought to land. They went by horse cart to a collective farm near Plotinnovo. They were welcomed there, and a kind peasant woman opened her house to Mother, Paul and Aino. Paul worked driving a team of horses, making hay on the farm. Mother and Aino cleaned, washed clothes, milked cows. There wasn't much food, because most of it was taken away for the soldiers, but at least people weren't starving there.

Paul, especially, was impressed by the little Russian village. The people there had what he called a "natural economy": Everything they needed they made at home, except salt, matches and gasoline. They cleaned their teeth with pine tar, made honey from the blossoms of linden trees and wove shoes from tree bark. At dinner, family members all ate from one common pot, and they looked with curiosity at the forks Paul and Aino and Mother had brought, and at all the plates.

The winter passed. They were safe. The war didn't touch them.

In the summer of 1942, Paul and most of the other men were sent to the city of Berezniki to construct an airplane factory. For him, the pleasant village life was over. He later told Mother that the men there worked long, hard days building the factory. At night, they slept in a barracks. There was no recreation. Food was plain and rations scanty. They grew even thinner. They were bone-tired all the time.

One night, long past midnight, the foreman burst into the barracks and woke the men. "Get up!" he yelled. "There's work to be done!" A trainload of materials had arrived, and the foreman wanted the men to jump up from their bunks and immediately unload the railroad cars. Paul was furious. It wasn't enough that they worked twelve hours a day. Now their sleep was to be interrupted as well? He and three of his friends refused to unload the rail cars.

The foreman was not used to defiance. He threatened Paul and the others with arrest. But by now, Paul had had his fill. All he wanted was to live a simple life, with enough to eat and a warm house to shelter him, away from the bustle of big cities and away from the corruption of the foremen and camp guards. He wanted to be where he could ski and hunt and fish and some day raise a family. He decided to head back to the collective farm where Mother and Aino were.

The next night, while the other men were sleeping, Paul and his three friends made their escape. They packed a leather bag with food and a change of socks and slipped out of the barracks. They walked for hours through the woods until they reached the banks of the Karma River. There, they traded the bag for a wooden boat, and as the sun came up, they floated away.

For twenty days they roamed, living on potatoes and vegetables they dug up from communal farms. "This is the Soviet Union," they joked to each other. "This food belongs to the people. We are people. These must be our potatoes." And in the dead of night, under cover of darkness, they dug up only enough potatoes to dull their hunger. Most days, they ate the potatoes raw, just brushing off the dirt.

They came to a bridge where two soldiers lounged, rifles slung carelessly over their shoulders, and they panicked. They decided to leave the water and take to the woods, so they traded the boat for two loaves of bread. Then they struck off through the trees. After walking for twenty days, they were back in Plotinnovo. They waited in the woods until dark, and then they slipped into their families' rooms.

Mother said she did the best she could to hide him. But someone was watching. Someone knew he was there. Two weeks later, Paul was called up to the Labor Army.

By this time—the end of 1942—the Soviet Union had two

armies. As a foreign-born, Paul, like thousands of others, wasn't trusted to fight with the Red Army at the front—especially not the Finnish front. Instead, he was sent to the Labor Army, which was no better than slavery. In the Labor Army, men didn't fight; they lived in squalor and starvation and worked constructing munitions plants, factories and airplanes. It didn't matter if the men had never worked construction before; they learned quickly, or died. Of all the grim and deadly labor camps sprinkled across the Soviet Union during World War II, Tchelyabinsk was, without a doubt, one of the worst.

And it was to Tchelyabinsk that they sent Paul.

Mother and Aino were sent further east, to a collective farm in the Perm region, near the Ural Mountains. Mother worked as a dairymaid, and Aino as a house cleaner. They were thin and hungry, not starving, but desperately malnourished. The food they were given was barely enough to keep them going, and at night they sometimes couldn't sleep, for worry over Paul and Father.

After many months, Paul got word to them. He had been worked nearly to death in the Labor Army and had been sent to a collective farm to recover. They wrote back immediately, but they didn't hear from him again for some time. The next time he wrote, he was in a hospital at Tchelyabinsk. It was there that I sent him the invitation, signed by the Karelian Council of Ministers, urging him to return home.

Mother and Aino weren't moved again. They stayed on the farm until they received my invitation, and then they joined me in Bielomorsk.

But what we all really wanted was to return to our old home, Petrozavodsk. As the Finnish army continued to retreat, we finally got the chance to do just that. The government moved back to Petrozavodsk, and we went with it. We packed our few clothes and caught the train for home. When we arrived, my mother began to weep. So many of the old wooden houses had been burned to the ground, and so many of the solid downtown buildings were now nothing more than piles of bricks and rubble. We didn't know it then, but it was the Soviets, not the Finns, who had destroyed the town, not wanting to leave anything of value for the enemy to use.

The symphony hall had been destroyed, and several blocks on the waterfront were now filled with waist-high weeds. The golden tansy and frilly Queen Anne's lace were fragrant and tenacious, pushing up from ground that was littered with broken bricks. The building my old room had been in was gone, and with it all the possessions I had left behind.

There was no use feeling sorry for ourselves; everyone was in the same boat. We found new quarters, and we began life again with nothing more than our empty hands. We had no dishes, no pots and pans, no tables or chairs. We slept on the floor at first. We lived like cave men.

The room we were assigned to had been vacated by a Karelian woman who had moved back into her parents' house. She saw that we had nothing, and she offered us a couple of chairs, a table and some kitchen utensils.

Aino took a job with the railroad. Her reasoning was sound: She would be issued a uniform, and that way she wouldn't have to worry about finding new clothes, so scarce in those days of war. She was assigned the Petrozavodsk–Leningrad run, and sometimes the Petrozavodsk–Georgia run, and every few weeks she came back with baskets heavy with fresh fruits and vegetables from the south.

By this time, the food situation had begun to improve. Lend-Lease, the American program set up to help the Allies, provided some food, and every now and then we were able to put together a treat—canned Spam, omelets made with powdered eggs, or pancakes made with American flour and fried in American lard.

But for Mother, it was too late. She had been malnourished for too many years, and she was completely worn out. She finally agreed to see a doctor, but the prognosis was grim. He didn't give her much time to live.

"That's nonsense, girls," she scolded as we brought her home again. "There's nothing wrong with me that a little rest and good food won't cure. I'll have one of those peaches that Aino brought home. That's just what I need." But though her words were brave, I could see the exhaustion in her face, and I knew that the doctor was right.

I wanted more than anything to write to her relatives; I knew that Mother would die happy if she had word from her sisters and brothers in Finland or the United States. She had heard nothing from them in so many years. But the borders were closed to all forms of travel and communication. Here in Stalin's Soviet Union, we lived in complete isolation from the rest of the world.

I continued as night editor at Tass, working until midnight or one each morning. The schedule worked well: I was around in the daytime to see to Mother's needs, and I went to work in the late afternoon, when she was napping. One of our neighbors, eighty-year-old Aura Kiiskinen, also dropped in several times a day to check on Mother.

Late one night in May 1945 I was preparing to switch off the equipment and head for home. The teletype had been silent for hours, and I had already sent all the news on to the local newspapers. But just as I was getting ready to leave, one last message came across the wires. "Remain open. Extraordinary news expected," it said. I turned the lights back on and notified the newspapers to hold the presses. And then I waited.

The news didn't come through until nearly three in the morning, and by then I could hear the beginnings of celebration in the streets outside. The war was over. The Nazis had surrendered. Our world was at peace.

I walked home along streets filled with dancing people. It wasn't yet dawn, but the news had already made its rounds. The streets, usually so silent at this time of night, were as crowded as on a sunny afternoon. The war was finally over! We could rebuild our city.

We could rebuild our country. Our friends and loved ones could come home. Our lives would return to normal.

But for us Corgans, it seemed, there was no normal. We still had no word from Father or Paul, and there would be no rejoicing for us until we did.

Months went by, and finally a friend of Paul's got word to us, telling us that Paul was in prison far to the east. I wrote a long petition to the Supreme Soviet, pleading for his release. But then we heard nothing more.

Mother died in the winter, early in the new year of 1946. It had been a hard winter for her, and she had begun to spend more and more time in bed with the covers tucked under her chin. For two months, she had been completely bedridden. It frightened me to see her lying there so still—my energetic mother, the woman whose hands were never idle, finally seemed content to lie for hours without moving.

She never spoke of Father or Paul—I think it was too painful for her—but one frigid morning, the first of February, 1946, she moved her head fretfully on the pillow and began to speak. Aino and I were at her side in an instant.

"It's all our fault," she said, plucking at the blanket with one thin hand. "Why did we come here? Where's Oscar? Where's Paul?" Aino and I looked at each other, frightened, unsure what to do. "It's a good thing that Leo is sleeping at home," Mother said. Her voice was weak. "It's a good thing that Leo never came here." And her big brown eyes filled with tears.

Mother died that afternoon. At the funeral home, we put her coffin on a sled and dragged it the whole way home. We had no car and no one to help us. Our tears turned to sleet on our cheeks as we pulled the heavy sled up the hill and along the river all the way to our house. Then we laid out our mother in the middle of our room.

For two days, the body of our mother lay in a coffin in our room, and we spent the night with neighbors. We didn't know how we were going to take her to the graveyard. No one we knew had a car. No one we knew even had a horse cart. The graveyard was far away, on the other side of town, and we knew we didn't have the strength to pull the coffin all the way there in the bitter cold. I don't know what we would have done if a government official hadn't come to our building. The elections were a few days away, and officials were going door to door, making sure that people voted. When the man knocked at our door, he found Aino and me, our eyes swollen from weeping, and our mother's coffin in the middle of our room.

"There's one of your citizens who won't be voting!" I said, pointing to Mother. We began to cry again.

The man was kind and told us not to worry. He promised to get a truck and take Mother to the graveyard for us, and he did. He drove us there himself, the next day. Only he, Aino and I and a handful of friends were there as Mother was lowered into the frozen ground.

Two weeks later, Paul came home.

He was dressed in rags, thin and frail, but we were glad to see him. It was so rare to have someone come home again from prison! We didn't ask him right away to relay his experience, but slowly, over the next few weeks, as he rested and we fed him nourishing soup and watched over him, Paul's story came out.

He began his story with his experiences in the notorious labor camp, Tchelyabinsk. The place was fenced with barbed wire, he said. Armed guards kept watch in guard towers, day and night. Paul was sent there in November.

The men slept in unheated dugouts in the freezing weather. They worked twelve hours a day. They dug trenches in the frozen ground with crowbars and shovels. They were given no socks, no coats, no warm clothes, no hot food. The temperature dipped to ten degrees below zero. Paul's boots had holes in them, and he froze his heels. They ate mostly bread and water. Men mixed the bread with the water so it would seem more filling. They drank water—quarts and quarts of water a day, in a desperate attempt to fill their stomachs and ease the gnawing pangs of hunger. They drank so much water they began to swell up and became very ill. Many people died.

By early spring of 1943, Paul was terribly weak. His weight had dropped from 160 pounds to less than 120. His face was as thin as a skull, and his calves and thighs became so wasted that his kneecap was the thickest part of his leg. The once healthy, handsome young man had become a skeleton, grown too weak even to walk. He lay in bed, surrounded by dying men. Finally, the weakest men were sent to a collective farm to recover. Paul went with them. It was there that he was finally able to write Mother.

Life on the collective farm did not help Paul. He was expected to work for his living, but he was too weak to lift a hoe or a rake. Finally, someone sent him to the Tchelyabinsk labor camp hospital, where German doctors—all prisoners of war—took pity on him. By then, Paul was delirious, tossing in his bed and muttering in English. The German doctors saved his life. They kept him in the hospital, giving him nourishing food and vitamins, and they held off the labor-camp guards by telling them that Paul was still unfit for physical work. Paul was allowed to rest in the hospital and regain some of his strength.

He was better, but still very weak, when word came that the Finns had pulled out of Petrozavodsk and the government was seeking residents to return to Karelia and help with the rebuilding of the republic. Paul received my invitation, and he made plans to return home. He got his documents together and boarded the train for Moscow. But his suffering wasn't over yet. On the train, two young soldiers stopped him, took away his papers and hauled him back to Tchelyabinsk. There was a quick trial, and Paul was sentenced to five years. His crime? Desertion.

Paul was in prison for more than a year. He was not allowed to write letters. None of us knew where he was. Finally, one of his friends from the Labor Army was able to get word to Petrozavodsk. When we heard of Paul's whereabouts, I wrote a long petition to the Supreme Soviet of the USSR. It was a miracle; the officials listened to my plea. Paul was summoned before the council. They pardoned him, gave him a train ticket to Petrozavodsk and money and food for the trip.

At the prison, the guards took the food and money away from him, but they left him his ticket and his papers. Paul didn't even protest. He was glad just to be going home. The trip from Tchelyabinsk to Moscow took three days, and the train was so crowded he had to stand the entire time. He had no food, but at the Moscow station he was able to get a drink of water. He helped an elderly woman with her baggage in Moscow, and she gave him a piece of bread. It was the only food he ate during the entire trip.

It took him seven more days to reach Petrozavodsk. The trains ran at odd times, and they were crowded with passengers. People hung on wherever they could. They stood, they sat on their bundles, they clung to the sides of cars. Everyone was going somewhere, but no one knew how long it would take to get there. Paul waited at the Moscow station day and night, never knowing when a train bound for Petrozavodsk might show up and never knowing whether he would be able to squeeze himself onto a car.

All this time, he ate nothing. He had no money, and no one had any food to spare. So he drank water, and he waited. A train finally came, and he found room. He was lightheaded from lack of food and grimy with soot. His stomach no longer hurt; he was beyond feeling hungry. It was evening when the train arrived in Petrozavodsk. Somehow, he found where we were living. Somehow, he made it to our room. He knocked on the door.

I was building a fire in the stove. I turned, a piece of wood in my hand, to see a filthy man leaning in our doorway. He was gaunt. His hair was long. His eyes glittered with hunger. I stared at him, unspeaking. I knew him, but I was too surprised to say a word.

Paul spoke for me. "Mayme," he said. "It's me."

No Tears Left

So many people had died.

We walked through the grim streets of Petrozavodsk, past the rubble and broken glass of demolished buildings, past the lines of people waiting to buy food, and we looked at faces, hoping to find someone we knew. But so many were gone. Some had died in battle, some during the evacuation, some in labor camps. Some, like my mother, held on until they could die at home.

Every week, nearly every day, I heard news of another friend who had not survived. Miriam Kupiainen, with whom I had lived when my family moved to Uhtua, had died during the evacuation. Vaino Rimpinen, with whom my family had stayed when we first moved to Brooklyn, died digging trenches near Petrozavodsk. Ruth Niskanen returned to find that her mother had died of hunger during the evacuation, and her brother had died in battle.

If you let yourself cry for one, soon you will find you have no tears left. We mourned those who were gone, welcomed the ones who returned and pressed on with our lives.

Paul moved in with Aino and me. The room was small and cramped, but it didn't matter. We had few possessions, and we were almost never all there at the same time. Aino's job on the railroad kept her away for days at a time.

Paul was gone a lot, too, working during the day and attending school at night. He took a job growing potatoes on the university farm and later started working at a local sawmill. He was quite thin and weak, but gradually he began to fill out and look like the Paul of old. He began to ski again in the winter, and the long cross-country afternoons added muscle to his emaciated body and color to his pale cheeks.

I had finished high school in 1945, the year I turned twenty-two. After Mother's death, I took some time off, but I resumed my studies in 1948. That year, a group of us from America—Ruth Niskanen, Helvi Finberg, Mary Haajanen and I—enrolled in the two-year teachers' college. Helvi, Mary and Ruth planned to teach English upon graduation, but I entered the program purely for the education. I already had a good career with Tass. The editors and officials in Moscow had commended me several times for my work, and I planned to live out my career as a journalist.

The rebuilding of Petrozavodsk continued. Slowly, broken bricks and rubble were hauled away, and workers began replacing some of the demolished buildings. Housing, though, was still scarce. The store shelves remained quite bare, though the economy began to improve and food prices dropped to more reasonable levels. It was still hard to get consumer goods; clothes, furniture, shoes and cooking utensils were nearly impossible to come by, and Paul, Aino and I used our wits to scrounge what we needed.

Gradually, we renewed friendships with people we had been separated from during the war. Although many had died, many had survived. We were gladdened every time we saw another familiar face. But in all this time, we had no word of Father.

It was in 1948 that I encountered a face from the past that filled me with joy: Milton Sevander, the musician from Petrozavodsk, who had vanished early in the war and whom we never expected to see again. At first, Milton kept his tragic war story hidden. He wasn't one to talk about his suffering, but it eventually became clear that he was deeply embittered by the events of the war.

Gradually, over the next few months, his story came out.

Milton Sevander had no love of battle. He was a trombone player, a charming, amiable young man, the son of a singer and an actress, and the nephew of an actor. Music and gaiety were in his blood, not battles and war. But he was also a brave man, and when he was called up, he did his duty.

He was twenty years old in 1940, the year he became a soldier in the Soviet Red Army. His unit served in Karelia, attempting to hold off the advance of the Finns.

But during the winter of 1942, Milton's partisan detachment met with disaster. After a battle, the men scattered into the forest. Some were wounded, most had lost their rations. They wandered for days through the frozen Karelian woods, lost, bleeding, disoriented from hunger. As cold and starvation took hold, some lay down in the snow and died. Others wandered off into the woods, never to be seen again.

Milton and another soldier stuck together. They dug in the deep drifts for frozen berries. They ate snow. Days turned into nights. They lost track of time and feared they were doomed to die in the glittering white forest.

When the Finnish army found them, they were near death. All the other men in their detachment had vanished. Milton and his friend were taken to Medvezhegorsk, which had fallen to the Finns. They were given something hot to drink, and then they were questioned. Both were sentenced to be executed at dawn.

The men were returned to their cells for their final night. Neither of them slept.

A few hours before dawn, an officer from the Finnish General Army Headquarters came by for a midnight inspection. When he discovered that Milton had been born in Eveleth, Minnesota, he immediately canceled Milton's execution.

"You're American-born," the officer said. "We have no argument with the Americans. Your life will be spared." And he sentenced Milton, instead, to life in prison.

But his friend was Finland-born. He was considered a traitor for emigrating to the Soviet Union and serving in its army. At dawn the next morning, Milton heard the shot that ended the man's life—a single shot that cracked through the cold morning and rang in his ears. In his cell, Milton held his head in his hands and fought back the tears.

Milton was sent to the prison in Riihimaki, Finland, where he expected to end his days. He was there for two years. In 1944, Finland dropped out of the war and settled its account with the Soviet Union. The two countries agreed to exchange prisoners, and Milton was brought back to the Soviet Union. But Stalin's philosophy prevailed: Anyone who had been captured was not to be trusted. Instead of getting the hero's welcome that he deserved, Milton was sent to a prison camp in Tkvibuli, Georgia. For four years, he slaved away in a coal mine, unable to leave, unable to communicate with his family. No one knew where he was. No one knew if he was alive or dead.

Finally, in 1948, he was sent home. He received no decorations, no honor for his bravery, no medals or ribbons or recognition. Four years in a prison camp, and nothing else. This was his reward for serving his country.

Milton and I had always been close, and his story touched me deeply. It wasn't long after his return to Petrozavodsk that we decided to marry.

People were married in those days for a number of reasons; love was only one of them. People married in order to get better housing, to move out of cramped, shared rooms, or to banish the demons of loneliness and fear the war had called up. Marriage, in the post-war Soviet Union, was as much a practical decision as it was a romantic one. There were no weddings then; society recognized marriage as a civil, rather than religious, event. To marry, a couple merely had to go downtown and sign an official document. Doves, cupids and lacy gowns had no place in our lives. The horrors we had endured during the purges and the war had stripped us of any romantic illusions.

Milton and I had no ceremony, no ritual and certainly no honeymoon, but we started our life together gladly and with the best wishes of our friends. He and I had always been deeply fond of each other, and we knew we would make a good couple. It pleased me to think that I would live in a house where there would always be music.

After the war, Petrozavodsk began to grow. Its population swelled from twenty thousand in 1944 to more than eighty thousand just six years later. Some of the fear that had permeated our lives during the purges lifted, but Stalin's repression and discrimination against people of different nationalities continued. We worked around it, trying to do our best to improve society and our own lives, and trying not to be held back too much.

My time was filled with working nights at Tass, attending day classes at the teachers' college, and building my life with Milton. And when I found I was pregnant in 1949, even that didn't slow me down.

That winter I was invited to a conference of Tass editors in Moscow. In the past I had loved visiting the capital, walking the bustling streets of the big city, strolling the Old Arbat and visiting the GUM department store. But I had never been to Tass headquarters, had never met the people I listened to on the radio, spoke with on the phone or communicated with over the teletype. So I was tempted to attend the conference, but it was late in my pregnancy, and it seemed more prudent to stay home.

My supervisor said he understood, but his wife wouldn't hear of it. "You have to go, Mayme; it won't be any fun without you," she said. "Here, I have something for you." And she brought out a warm, white wool shawl and draped it over my shoulders. "You just stay wrapped up in this, and no one will even notice you're pregnant," she said. And so I went.

It was early December. Streetcars clacked past on the snowy Moscow streets, and crowds of people pushed and jostled along the sidewalks. St. Basil's Cathedral was lit up, its onion domes colorful and dramatic against the snow, and the line at Lenin's tomb stretched across Red Square, the people waiting patiently to view the body of their leader as the snowflakes melted on their cheeks and eyelashes.

The officials at Tass greeted me warmly, and I was finally able to assign faces to the voices I had heard so many times over the years. On one afternoon we all toured the Kremlin, and I wandered with awe through the hallways where so many important people had walked.

Of course, security was tight, and at each checkpoint the officials scrutinized our passports. When they realized I was American-born, they looked me up and down and whispered among themselves, but I just stood there in my coat and big white shawl, waiting, and finally they let me pass.

Our daughter was born January 2, 1950. We named her Stella, after my long-ago friend from New York, Stella Baker. Our baby was just a tiny thing, wrinkled and red but with a strong, lusty cry, and I knew she was going to be a child with a will of her own. I was glad because strong people are survivors. I wished my parents could have seen her, their first grandchild, and I promised myself that Stella would grow up knowing the story of her grandparents and their tragic attempt to help improve the world.

In the Soviet Union, women are given four months of maternity leave with full pay, but I couldn't stay away from work for that long because there was no one at Tass to replace me. Stella was a good baby—not much work, though even at this young age she made her opinions known. While she slept, I paced our room and worried about how my work was getting done at Tass. I returned to my job when Stella was just a few weeks old and proceeded to wear myself out caring for her, cooking, shopping, attending teachers' college and working.

Milton pitched in and did what he could, but between rehearsals and concerts he was busy, too, and I began to wonder how we were ever going to manage. I knew that I did not want to repeat my mother's life, sacrificing everything for my family, but I also wanted my family to be safe and well cared for. The answer appeared on our doorstep one afternoon in the person of Milton's mother, Lillian. She had left her job at the printing house, she told me, to tend to Stella. If we wanted her, she was at our disposal. Lillian's help made our lives much easier, and I was able to finish my coursework at the teachers' college and receive my diploma that summer.

My first experience in front of a classroom came during my last term of college, when we were all required to practice teach. I was assigned to School No. 9, and I showed up more than an hour early. I wasn't nervous, exactly, but I was anxious to do a good job. I knew English well, but would I be able to teach it well? When I walked into the faculty lounge, my anxieties were forgotten. There, sitting at the table, sipping a glass of tea, was Ludmila Ivanovna, my old teacher from my first Russian school. I walked over to her and held out my hand. "Do you remember me?" I asked.

She peered at me through her thick spectacles. "Mayme Corgan!" she said, and I was encouraged at her warm smile. "Well, what in the world are you doing here?"

"I'm teaching English," I said. "I'm in my last quarter at the teachers' college."

"Sit down," she said, making room for me beside her. "Tell me what you've been doing all these years. How did your family weather the war?"

I told her about exile to Latushka, and how the war had separated my family. But when I started telling her about my job at Tass, she interrupted me. "Who has taught you Russian?" she asked. "Your Russian is so good."

"You did, Ludmila Ivanovna," I said. "Only you."

She shook her head in amazement. "I said you'd never learn Russian. This is hard to believe."

"There is no language a person cannot learn if they try very hard," I said. "I had good basic instruction from you, and I kept on practicing even after I had to leave school."

Ludmila Ivanovna rose to return to the classroom. "You cannot know how happy your words have made me," she said. "I am pleased beyond belief to see how well your Russian has progressed. I hope that you have equal success with your own students!" She pressed my hand warmly and left the room.

Practice teaching went well. I found that I enjoyed being in front of the classroom and felt quite comfortable teaching. It was a pleasant alternative to being a student myself and an enjoyable interlude from my work at Tass. But even so, when practice teaching was over and I received my diploma, I figured that that part of my life was behind me now. Teachers' college had been good training, but I still wanted a university education. I hadn't forgotten my promise to my parents. *Gems of the World's Best Classics* had been lost forever during the war, but what it represented lived on.

I knew that I couldn't attend college in Moscow or Leningrad. Moscow was so far away that it was out of the question—I had a family now, and responsibilities—and as an American-born Finn, I was not allowed to live and study in Leningrad. But I knew there was more than one way to accomplish my goal. Helvi, Mary, Ruth and I decided to study through correspondence courses.

The Leningrad Pedagogical Institute accepted all four of us at the third-year level, and we immediately began our studies. The correspondence course required that we attend lectures for two weeks every winter and for five weeks every summer, and that we take our examinations in person. In between, we could continue to work and live at home in Petrozavodsk. Within three years, we were told, we would receive our degrees.

My brother Paul was still single and had fewer obligations. He wanted to devote himself full-time to his studies, but he met with the same discrimination that the rest of us had experienced. Leningrad University turned down his application, telling him that as a Finn he was not allowed to live in Leningrad. And then Petrozavodsk University turned down his application to their geology program. Who knows what secrets they thought Paul might reveal, and to whom he might reveal them?

The paranoia was pervasive and ridiculous, but Paul had no choice but to change his plans. Undaunted, he applied to enter Petrozavodsk University's hydromechanics program and he was accepted. He began teaching mathematics in night school to support himself.

That summer everything seemed sunny and blooming. The economy was improving, and goods were more abundant in the stores. Milton performed in some important concerts, Stella was thriving and I was promoted to head of the Foreign and Soviet News Department at Tass. I had four or five people working under me, and I was responsible for every word of news that we released. It was a tremendous responsibility, and I took my work very seriously. But the sunshine couldn't last forever. Dark clouds rolled in that summer when our director at Tass was promoted to the Leningrad bureau. His replacement was Alexei Shvaryov, a hard-liner and a strict Stalinist who came from our republic's newspaper, *Leninskaya Pravda.*

On his second or third day on the job, he summoned me into his office. "We have a shortage of Finnish translators here," he told me. "I've decided to transfer you to the translating department."

I protested. My Finnish wasn't good enough; I had had only two years of formal Finnish schooling, and that had been years ago. And besides, I loved what I was doing. I didn't want to change. "Translating is a serious business," I said. "One mistake, and I could change the meaning of an entire story. I'm much more comfortable staying where I am, and I'm sure I'm much more valuable to Tass here, as well."

One of the men in the translating department spoke up. In just a few weeks, he said, he could have me reading, writing and translating Finnish like a native. I shook my head. Between my studies and my family, I had a heavy load, and I didn't want to take on new burdens. Alexei Shvaryov said nothing, but I could tell by the look on his face that he was not happy with my refusal.

For the next few weeks, he ignored me, and I assumed that if I worked hard and did my job well, the whole thing would blow over. But one day, at the end of July, I was summoned to his office again. I had been at work the night before until two in the morning and had come back to work at nine o'clock. Besides that, my few hours of sleep had been interrupted by a crying baby because Stella was teething. I was bone-tired and in no mood for nonsense when I went into his office. He didn't invite me to sit down. He didn't even greet me at all. He merely looked up from his desk and barked, "You're fired."

I blinked. "What?" I asked. I knew I had heard him correctly, but his words didn't register; I had been a loyal, hard-working employee of Tass for years, and I had certainly done nothing to warrant dismissal.

"You're fired," he said, and I could tell he relished the moment.

"What for?"

"Your biography is not in order," he said, leaning back in his chair and pressing his fingertips together. "It has too many black spots on it. We cannot keep you here."

I knew he was referring to my father's arrest, and his cruel words went straight to my heart. "Well," I said, and I made my voice as icy as I could. "That's very interesting. I've never heard anything of the kind." And I turned on my heel and walked out of his office. The headquarters of the Central Committee of the Communist party was not far away, and I marched straight to their office and asked to see the secretary of the Department of Propaganda.

Once in his office, I found myself trembling in anger. I took a deep breath to calm myself. "What kind of a country do we live in?" I asked him. The secretary of propaganda looked startled. "What do you mean?" he said, and I realized that orders for my dismissal had not come from him.

"I was just fired," I said. "I have been with Tass since I was seventeen years old, and I've just been fired. I was told that my biography isn't in order."

"That's impossible," he said, frowning. "There must be some mistake."

"Yes, there's certainly been a mistake," I agreed. "I can bring you a stack of commendations from Moscow for my work. Nobody has ever said one word against my work. And now this stuff about black spots on my biography. . . ." My voice shook. "Nobody has the right to insult me or anyone else like this."

"This is all a misunderstanding," the secretary said soothingly. "The director is new here. He doesn't understand. We'll fix this up. Don't you worry."

I nodded and returned to my office. Within the hour, my telephone rang. It was my supervisor, but this time he didn't summon me; he just gave me the news over the phone. "Well, you can have your job back," he said, and I noted with satisfaction that he sounded demoralized. I imagined that the secretary of propaganda must have given him quite a dressing-down.

But even as he offered to let me keep my job, an idea was forming in my head. I know I surprised him with my response. "Take my job back?" I said, a tone of polite surprise in my voice. "What, and work for *you*? No, thank you." There was a baffled silence on the other end of the phone, and I pressed on. "I don't want my job back. But there are some things I do want: I want my vacation pay, and I want the extra month's salary that's due me, and I want them by the end of the week."

I hung up the phone, pulled on my sweater, and walked across the square to the ministry of education. Since the war, the entire

Soviet Union had been short of teachers, and they welcomed me with open arms. Even on short notice, they had a place for me. I took the next four weeks off to spend with my family, and on August 31, I reported for duty. I was now a fifth-grade English teacher at School 22.

To Know the Truth

Mournful organ music throbbed outside the window of our room. The loudspeakers were broadcasting Bach.

For two days, this melancholy music played over all the radios, over all the loudspeakers in town, without explanation. The drab March streets were made even gloomier by the heavy dirges and mournful chords. For two days and nights we listened to this music until we thought we would weep from the somberness of it all. And then on March 7, 1953, we finally were told the news: Josef Stalin was dead.

I'd been teaching for more than two years, and Milton was still playing in the orchestra. Stella was a pudgy blonde toddler, curious and energetic. I was pregnant again, in my seventh month, and starting to feel bulky and sluggish, but the day I heard the news about Stalin, I flew to work as if on wings.

Despite the oppressive music and gray, slushy snow, I felt as lighthearted and cheerful as if it were spring. *Things will change now,* I kept thinking. *Things will get better. Perhaps I'll be able to start writing to my cousins and friends in Finland, Sweden and America; perhaps this terrible, oppressive isolation we all live under will end. And perhaps,* I even allowed myself to think, *perhaps now Father will be released from prison.*

When I arrived at school to find teachers weeping in each other's arms, I was surprised. For decades, Stalin had blanketed the country with portraits and statues of himself, and *Pravda* had devoted endless column inches to glorifying his name, but I never thought anyone actually believed such propaganda. Nearly everywhere I looked, I saw red eyes and worried faces.

In the school's gym, a gigantic portrait of Stalin was hanging on the wall, surrounded with flowers and funeral wreaths. Honor guards stood on either side. Students and teachers filed past the portrait one at a time, laying flowers and wiping away tears. Although I declined to take my turn, I tried not to betray my real feelings in any way.

Perhaps we Finns were more clear-eyed. Perhaps coming from another country gave us a better perspective, because most of my American-Finnish friends felt the same sense of relief that I did. For the most part, though, the nation was plunged into grief. From all over the Soviet Union, packed trains carried mourners to Moscow, people clinging to the roofs and doorways of rail cars. At Stalin's funeral, hundreds of people were killed, trampled to death by the crowds as they surged forward, desperate to glimpse his body. These were the last victims of Stalin—the faithful, the mourners.

Our son, Leo, was born on May 27. Twenty days later, I boarded the train for Leningrad with Leo in my arms to take my final examinations. The summer before, Ruth, Mary, Helvi and I had found an apartment to stay in while we attended the five-week summer course. But toward the end of our stay, we had been found out. Ruth had fallen ill with appendicitis, and we had summoned a nurse to our room. The nurse treated Ruth, but she also turned us in to the police.

It was still illegal for ethnic Finns to live in Leningrad, even for just a few weeks, and we were ordered to vacate the apartment immediately and return home. We were terrified, but stubborn: we had put too much into our studies to halt them now. We promised the officials that we would leave immediately, but instead we dimmed the lights and hid in the dark all night. The next morning we stopped at the institute, took our examinations, and then boarded the train for home.

This summer was easier, though I had an infant to care for. No one bothered us, and at the end of our five weeks, we received our diplomas. At long last, I was university educated. I knew that my father would have been proud, if only there was some way to let him know.

At this time I did not belong to the Communist party. I still believed fervently in socialism. I still tried to live up to the ideals of my father. But at the same time, I doubted that the Soviet Union was being run by those principles. At a party earlier that summer, a friend and I got into an argument about communism. I knew that it was risky to speak out, and I knew that anyone at the party might twist my words and get me into trouble, but I've never been one to keep my opinions to myself.

What troubled me the most was the privileged system under which high-ranking party members lived. Clearly, they enjoyed a lifestyle that the rest of us could only dream about. They had automobiles, good quality clothing, plenty of food and access to shops that we were banned from. For us, consumer goods remained in short supply, and what there was was flimsy and shoddy.

I couldn't understand it; before the war, I had bought a pair of shoes in Leningrad that were the finest shoes I had ever seen. They were beautiful and comfortable, and they held up through many snowy winters and rainy summers. But now, goods were poorly made. The shoes I saw for sale were ugly and clunky and fell apart after the first good rain. I knew that Russians were capable of making good products, as they had before the war. Why weren't they now?

I knew that the only way to have any influence over the future of the country—or my own future—was as a party member, but still I hesitated to join. I didn't want any part of the special favors. I wanted to work for the ideals I had been raised with. For weeks and months, I wrestled with the question of whether or not to join the Communist party. And I talked it over with my friends.

"How can you account for the fact," I asked a friend, "that when my father joined the party he gave up half his salary? And now people join the party to double their salaries. That's not the way it's supposed to be."

"No, no," my friend said. "You don't understand. It's the ruling party. And since they are ruling, they should get more money."

It made sense to him, but to me it was clearly wrong. The idea of workers being on the bottom tier and rulers being on the top was the opposite of what socialism stood for, the exact opposite of what my father believed in. It became clearer and clearer that the Soviet Union was based not on socialism, but on something else. For lack of another name, my friends and I called it "sovietism," and most of us did not agree with it. I kept up my membership in the Komsomol, but I held back in joining the Communist party.

With Stalin's death, though, there was a change in the country, a thawing, and I began to reconsider. Stalin was replaced by Nikita Khrushchev, a Ukrainian man with a head like a potato, but a good mind and heart. The country began to relax; there was a new feeling of hope in the air. Some of our fears dissipated, and people began to breathe a little more freely. Still, we were wary. Twenty-five years of Stalinism had taught us to keep our thoughts and feelings hidden to all but the most trusted of friends.

And then, three years after Stalin's death, Khrushchev gave a speech that sent shock waves throughout the country.

Khrushchev delivered the speech in February 1956 to the 20th Party Congress of the Soviet Union. The speech wasn't published, but it was read aloud to large audiences who gathered in public halls and auditoriums to listen. I heard it read in the auditorium

of the Pedagogical Institute. As Khrushchev's speech revealed
Stalin's unconscionable betrayals and atrocities, I listened, aghast,
and felt shock sweep through the room like a physical presence.

In his speech, Khrushchev outlined how Stalin had systemati-
cally and methodically eliminated all party members and high-
ranking government officials who disagreed with him—or whom
he thought disagreed with him. Thousands upon thousands of
people had died at Stalin's hands, Khrushchev told the country,
and thousands more had been imprisoned and tortured on no
evidence at all.

"Stalin originated the concept of 'enemy of the people,'"
Khrushchev said in his speech. "This term made possible the usage
of the most cruel repression, violating all norms of revolutionary
legality, against anyone who in any way disagreed with Stalin. . . .
The only proof of guilt used, against all norms of current legal
science, was the confession of the accused himself, and, as subsequent probing proved, confessions were acquired through physical pressures against the accused."

"Violating all norms of revolutionary legality" meant that Stalin
had felt himself above the law. "Physical pressures" meant torture.
As the speech went on, it became clearer and clearer what a monster
we had had as our leader—a monster, whom trusting people had
believed in the way people believe in God.

The speech took more than four hours to read, and when it was
over, I felt completely drained. Though Khrushchev's talk dealt
only with high-ranking party officials and not with rank-and-file
members like my father, it was clear that my father's fate had been
no different from the fate of the thousands of officials that he
mentioned.

As the speech went on, I felt relief at first, and then anger and
betrayal, and finally a deep unutterable sadness sweep over me.
What a relief, to finally understand my father's fate, and how
comforting to have it proven beyond a shadow of a doubt that he
was a victim of his times! For though our family had never doubted

him, not for a minute, we were still aware that a black cloud hung over his name. And now Khrushchev's speech made it clear that that black cloud was undeserved.

But still, how terribly, terribly sad to know that the night he was dragged away from his little house in Uhtua was the last time he was ever to see freedom. How sad to think that the hope we had clung to for so long—the hope that our father would be released from prison some day—would now never come true. For it was almost certain, now, that Father was dead. Khrushchev made it clear that Stalin's preferred method was to arrest a person, torture him in order to get him to betray others, and then have him shot. I prayed that my father's torture—if he had been tortured—had been brief. But I knew that nothing would ever have made my father betray anyone else.

I knew that I had to discuss Khrushchev's speech with Paul and Aino. By now, Paul had graduated from the university and was working in Lahdenpohja, a small town in Karelia. He was both math teacher and principal at the school there. He had married, and his wife, Bertha, also taught math. Aino had married, too, and was still working on the railroad, and the three of us no longer had the time to get together very often. But after Khrushchev's speech, we all met in Petrozavodsk to discuss the situation. We decided to apply to the government to learn Father's fate. Only then we would know for sure.

I sent an application to the Supreme Court of the U.S.S.R. It took several months for the reply, because the office was flooded, I'm sure, with thousands of other requests. I know that most of my friends had written. For nearly twenty years, we had all been haunted by the uncertain fate of our loved ones, and we all wanted to know the truth, terrible though it might be.

The reply was waiting for me one afternoon when I came home from school, and I opened it with trembling fingers. Inside was a rehabilitation paper for my father—proof positive that he was dead. On the basis of that document, I applied to the Civil

Registration Office and received his death certificate. It gave no place of burial, but said only that he had died of cancer in 1940. In my heart I had already known he was dead, but when I read that paper I began to weep, thinking of my strong, brave father, wasting away in a dark Soviet prison cell for years, his body eaten by cancer, with no word of love or support from his wife or children.

But Paul was not convinced the certificate told the entire truth. "Father was never sick a day in his life," he told me when I showed it to him. "The Corgans were all strong, healthy people. They all lived to a ripe old age. It just doesn't sound right that he would have died of cancer." But we had no way of knowing; we had no choice but to accept what the government had told us.

One by one, our friends began receiving information on their fathers, mothers, brothers and husbands. All the certificates said the same thing: the men were dead, and they had all died of natural causes—dysentery, or stomach ulcers, or pneumonia, or cancer. It didn't ring true, that so many men would have fallen mortally ill in prison, but there was no one for us to challenge.

At least we knew our father was no longer among the living. At least we didn't have to lie awake nights, worrying about him and wondering when we would see him again. We knew now that we never would. We finally knew that our father was gone forever.

Faces From the Past

I was only ten years old when my family moved to the Soviet Union. I was fourteen when my father was arrested, twenty-two when my mother died and just twenty-nine when the Stalin era ended. A lifetime of heartbreak was packed into those nineteen years.

But I do not want you to come away from this memoir pitying me. I do not want you to think that our lives were terrible. They were not. We endured great tragedies, it's true, and hardships almost beyond belief, but we also had success and happiness. We learned to be content with little, to find the good among the bad. Most of us became very pragmatic people. We had to, to survive.

We American Finns were not beaten down by the purges, exile, famine or war. Oh, a few were. Some turned to drink, some collapsed in other ways. But most of us were tough and resilient people; we built the best lives we could, and we did not complain.

After Stalin's death, our load grew lighter. Most of us went on to live happy, productive lives. The war years dimmed, and while we never forgot those who died, we put the past behind us and worked toward a better future. Socialism remained our dream, though it was clear that the country was being governed under a vastly corrupted version of socialism. We wanted no control, no special privileges, none of the power that Sovietism offered. We wanted only to build honest, productive lives for ourselves and each other. And, for the most part, that is what we did.

During the years of isolation, the arms buildup, McCarthyism and the Cold War, there were terrible misconceptions between the United States and the Soviet Union. We American-born Soviets knew the truth about America, but most Soviet citizens did not. Most Soviets believed that the United States was evil and that Americans wanted to dominate the world. They had no way of knowing how friendly and optimistic American people really are.

And most Americans, in turn, were taught to fear the Soviet Union. They considered our country to be a dark, mysterious place run by evil and fueled by dreams of power and war. Americans seldom visited our country. They had no way of knowing how World War II had destroyed our cities and devastated our people. They didn't know that we had erected monuments to fallen soldiers in every town, in every school building, in every city square. These were active monuments, monuments we visited often, even forty years after the war had ended. Some memorials burned with eternal flames, and others were decorated regularly with fresh flowers. War had killed millions of Soviet citizens. Millions died in battle and millions more died under siege and in evacuation. Our country wanted no part of another war. In our country, we were devoted to peace. But you in America had no way of knowing this.

Americans also believed that the Soviet people lived in constant persecution and oppression, lacking even basic freedoms. But that is not entirely true. Yes, most of us were wary and fearful of the KGB, the internal police force that had grown far too powerful. And yes, the Brezhnev years were, without question, repressive and harsh. But even so, day-to-day life in the Soviet Union after the Stalin era was not so different from life in other countries. We experienced the same joys and sorrows that people experience anywhere: births, deaths, marriages, the greetings and farewells that mark a full and rich existence.

Though my life in Russia began with tragedy, the last forty years have been relatively peaceful. I built a wonderful life surrounded by family and friends. I taught hundreds of Petrozavodsk young people to speak English and have been made proud almost daily by the accomplishments of my former pupils. My love for the theater and music grew, and my friendships with actors and musicians flourished.

I grieved when Milton died of a heart attack in 1973, and rejoiced when my two children, Stella and Leo, found mates of their own. And eventually I was blessed with grandchildren: Leo's two beautiful blonde children, whose broad faces and blue eyes proclaim their Finnish heritage, and Stella's lively, dark-haired boy, who shows the Russian roots of his father.

My brother and sister have done well for themselves, as well. Aino gave birth to a son, and Paul and Bertha have three children.

And most of us, the survivors of the original band of six thousand Finns, held true to the socialist creed that brought our families to the Soviet Union: to help our neighbors, be honest and true, share what we have with those who are less fortunate, and value people and cooperation above material wealth.

After Stalin's death, Petrozavodsk continued to grow and change. Modern buildings were put up, and in 1957 our family moved to an apartment on the fifth floor of a new high-rise on Lenin Street, not far from the city center. It was much larger than anywhere else we had lived in the Soviet Union—three rooms and a kitchen, with central heating and running water. It took another twenty-five years before the building added capacities for gas cooking and hot water, but finally, in 1983, I could tell my children that we now had the same luxuries the Corgan family had left behind in the United States back in 1934.

In 1960, I joined the Communist party. I believed in Khrushchev's integrity, and I decided that to turn my back on the Soviet Union and the great experiment of communism would be a betrayal of my father's memory. Khrushchev understood that Stalinism had nearly destroyed the country, and he worked to mend relations with the West. During his tenure, life grew better. Consumer goods improved, censorship relaxed and some of us were even allowed to travel.

My decision to join the party also was prompted by the fact that it was always the party secretary at any school or factory who had the most influence and could get the most done. I had ideas of my own that I wanted to put into practice, and I didn't want anybody telling me what I could or couldn't do.

It was during this time that I became interested in helping the Soviet Union build friendships with other countries. We knew that the Western world did not look favorably on communism or our country, and I wanted to do my part to build understanding. By now I could speak Swedish, as well as Finnish, English and Russian, and my knowledge of languages put me in a natural situation to help forge ties with people of other countries.

In 1962, a group of us from Petrozavodsk took our first trip abroad in thirty years. We went to Finland, my mother's homeland. We were excited, but apprehensive, about the trip. Our country's relations with Finland had been strained, at best, ever since Finland declared its independence from us in 1917. But to our amazement, we were welcomed everywhere we went—in cities like Helsinki, Tampere and Turku, as well as the smaller communities in the countryside. There were always scores of people to meet us, and bands playing, and gifts of fresh fruits and flowers. Such an outpouring of friendship and enthusiasm was overwhelming. There were no recriminations against those of us who were of Finnish heritage. There was no vestige of resentment against the battles fought during the Winter War or World War II.

The people who greeted us at train stations across Finland were members of a group we had never heard of before: The Finland-Soviet Friendship Society. At the end of our trip, as our train chugged north again toward Petrozavodsk, I thought about how wonderful it would be if we could start a similar group at home, encouraging exchanges and understanding between our two countries. And it occurred to me how fortunate it was that I had joined the Communist party, because I could use my influence as a party member to improve our international relations. I might not be able to do much for the country as a whole, but I could do one small part for Petrozavodsk, and for Karelia.

I told Peter Martinov, the head of the Propaganda and Agitation Department of the Regional Party Committee, about our experiences in Finland. "We, too, should have such a friendship society in Petrozavodsk," I told him, and he agreed.

"We have actually been thinking about this for some time," he said. Soviet red tape being what it is—lengthy and entangling—no one had acted on the idea. My suggestion prompted him, and within a short time, Martinov had formed a friendship society board and appointed me to it. I served on that board for the next twenty-five years.

In October 1964, the country went through another coup and Khrushchev was removed from power. Apparently, his interest in reform wasn't shared by other high-ranking members of the Politburo. He was replaced by the hard-liner, Leonid Brezhnev, a dull man with a broad Russian face and unfriendly eyes. We began to fear that the repression of the Stalin era might return. Brezhnev, it became clear, was no intellectual giant and was easily manipulated by others with more intelligence and ambition.

Some of our fears were founded; it's true that corruption flourished during the Brezhnev years and the Cold War chilled to its most frigid. But the door of freedom, once opened, can rarely be slammed completely shut again. We lived with oppression under Brezhnev, but things did not return to what they had been under Stalin.

I continued to work hard at my career, and eventually I was promoted to school principal. I later moved to the Pedagogical Institute to teach English. My involvement in foreign language clubs and friendship societies also continued. As Petrozavodsk began to establish sister cities in Scandinavia and Eastern Europe, I served on the committees and translated for Finnish and Swedish tourists.

During all this time, in the back of my mind, I held on to one more dream: the dream of returning to America—not to live (that, to me, would be a betrayal of everything my father had lived and died for) but to visit the country where I had been born. My father's and mother's sisters still lived on farms outside of Superior, and I wanted to visit them, to see how the country had changed in forty years, and to tell them in person the sad news of my parent's deaths.

After Khrushchev took power, our isolation lifted a little and I began corresponding with a few old friends in the United States. The mail was terribly slow, but it usually got through and it wasn't always censored.

In 1973, a friend in Sacramento, California, sent me an official invitation to visit the U.S., and that July I found myself flying across the world to the country of my birth. I had been curious about California ever since the year my father was offered a job there, and sometimes I wondered how different our lives would have been, had he accepted that appointment.

That trip was like a brief miracle. California was beautiful—warm and sunny and lush, and I met many wonderful people there, including Aunt Anna and her family who had moved to California. Members of the local Kiwanis Club invited me to speak at one of their meetings, and I found myself in the position of unofficial envoy for the Soviet Union. I tried to be truthful and tell them not only of the hard life there, but also of the fervent principles of the people who lived there, and how they wanted peace and prosperity for all.

Toward the end of my trip, I was invited to Superior to visit my cousins, Florence Pettingill and Raymond and Leonard Lindgren. They were the children of my father's sister, Eva, and I remembered them from a lifetime ago, when I was just a wide-eyed child. Ours was a bittersweet reunion. It was wonderful to be able to see each other again, but it was heart-breaking to have to tell them the news of their uncle's death. My Uncle Peter's daughter, Irene, who had lived with my family in Superior, and Irene's older sister, Clara, also came to see me.

Together, we members of the Corgan clan went to the Greenwood Cemetery outside of Superior. I laid flowers on my brother Leo's grave, and they laid flowers, as well, in memory of my father.

During the 1960s, 1970s, and 1980s, the Soviet Union went through a yo-yo-like progression of rulers: hard-liners like Brezhnev were replaced by more reasonable leaders, like Petrozavodsk's own Yuri Andropov.

Andropov, who had headed the KGB for many years, was a conservative man who approached change in a most cautious manner, but I am convinced that he was sincerely interested in reform. If only he had lived longer, I think he would have done great things. Of course, he also left behind the bloody legacy of Afghanistan, and for that, we can never forgive him.

It wasn't until 1985, when Mikhail Gorbachev took the reins of power, that we felt the fresh winds of change sweep the country. Gorbachev made it clear that he was truly interested in reform, and it was under his leadership that long-hidden truths—such as the realities of the Winter War and the atrocities of Stalin's death camps—were revealed.

It was during Gorbachev's time that we were allowed to read what the rest of the world had been reading for years, such as the works of Russian writers like Alexander Solzhenitsyn and Roy

Medvedev. They had written extensively—Medvedev from an historian's point of view, and Solzhenitsyn from a novelist's—about the realities of Stalin's gulags and labor camps, and I found their words both fascinating and chilling. How was it possible that such things had happened? How could we not have known?

The thought of my father living under such barbaric conditions for so many years prompted me to write a second time for a death certificate. Paul's doubts that Father had died of cancer had haunted me for years, and I now felt that if anyone was going to tell us the truth, it would be Gorbachev. So once again, I applied for a death certificate, and once again, I waited.

This time, though, I waited in fear. I was terrified at what I might find out. Perhaps Father hadn't died of cancer; perhaps he had died of torture. I had read about one prisoner who was ripped apart by feral dogs and other prisoners who were burned with cigarettes and had their bones broken, one by one. I didn't know how I could bear it if I found out that this had been my father's fate. It was almost easier not to inquire, but it is always best to know the truth, no matter how difficult it might be to endure.

My father's second death certificate arrived in the mail one afternoon in 1991. Again, it gave no place of burial. But it did say this: Oscar Corgan was arrested on November 4, 1937, and executed on January 8, 1938. He had not endured years and years of isolation and torture. He had not died a slow, painful death from cancer. He had been shot by a firing squad two months after his capture.

He had died a martyr to his beliefs, betrayed by the country he had believed in so fervently.

I was filled with relief to find out the truth about my father—relief that his suffering had, at least, been relatively brief. And I was filled anew with the desire to carry on his beliefs, to work as hard as I could to improve the Soviet Union—not to follow the party line, but to carry again the banner of labor and real, democratic socialism.

And now my life has come full circle.

On a summer morning in 1986, I stopped by the Petrozavodsk government building to drop off a translation I had done for the city council. As I waited to meet with the deputy minister, I noticed a document on a nearby desk. The words, "Duluth, Minnesota," jumped out at me, and I asked if I could read it.

It was a warm and friendly letter from a citizens group in the United States requesting that Duluth and Petrozavodsk become sister cities. Sister cities! Not only was it amazing to think of the United States and the Soviet Union becoming friends in this way, but the fact that the invitation was from my childhood home was nearly incredible.

My hand holding the Telex message trembled as I read on. The letter spoke of the sincere desire to improve relations between the two superpowers, and it talked about the similarities that made our two cities such a good match. Both Duluth and Petrozavodsk are on the edge of great lakes, the letter said. Both are surrounded by pine and birch forest, and both economies rely on papermaking, shipping, mining, tourism and timber. Both cities have Finnish-speaking populations. All sound reasons for a sister city relationship, to be sure. But the letter said nothing of the best reason of all: It said nothing of the hundreds of Minnesotans now living in Karelia. It said nothing of the native-born Americans transplanted to Petrozavodsk. Time and isolation had done their damage. We American Finns had been forgotten.

Memories of Superior, Wisconsin, flooded my brain as I stood at the department head's desk—not memories of my brief visit in 1973, but memories of my childhood there: our little apartment above *Tyomies,* of the Virginia cooperative store where my father had worked, of the Iron Range Finn Halls we visited, and of the rallies we attended at the Civic Center in downtown Duluth.

The document asked permission for the citizens group to visit Petrozavodsk that fall. My heart was filled with excitement and sadness at the same time. "Have you answered this request?" I asked. The department head shook his head. "No," he said. "We really didn't know what to make of it. This has been on my desk for months."

"You must write back! You must accept!" I said. "Don't you know that many of our citizens were born in Duluth, or near there? I myself was born just a few miles away." He didn't know. No one seemed to know. The history of our little band of six thousand Finns was being forgotten, swallowed up in the larger history of the Soviet Union. It was clear that this amazing coincidence, this fortuitous opportunity to remember, must not pass by.

Pyotr Fedorovich Ureznetsov, Karelian Minister Council foreign department head, came to the rescue. Soon he, Mayor Pavel Peshchenko and other city officials began preparing for the Duluthians' visit. Everyone was excited at the thought of Americans visiting our out-of-the-way city. Travel had only just begun to open up to the Soviet Union, and most visitors went no farther than Moscow or Leningrad.

We American Finns, grown old but still with vivid memories of Minnesota, Michigan and Wisconsin, also began to prepare for the visit. Ruth Niskanen, retired but still doing translation work; Ernest Haapaniemi, a Michigan logger now from the Karelian lumber camp of Matrosa; Wilhelm Niemi, with a head full of memories from his International Falls boyhood—one by one, the surviving American Finns tidied their apartments, laid in a supply of vodka, caviar and tea, bought bouquets of gladiola and carnations from the marketplace, and waited for the visitors.

The Duluthians arrived on a foggy morning in early September 1986. Dozens of us were there on the Petrozavodsk train platform, waiting for them in the misty dawn. It was quite early, but we were all wide awake. We had been far too excited to sleep. Plans had been laid for the Americans to visit our schools, daycare centers, our beloved Finnish theater, the Yuri Andropov Pioneer Palace, and dozens of other thriving, successful places that we former Americans had helped build. Our city had planned concerts, a dance, a meeting with the mayor, an evening with the city's intelligentsia.

Most exciting of all were the plans in place for the guests' last night: We American Finns would be taking them to our own homes and apartments to show them how we lived, and to talk and reminisce and swap stories about America.

A light rain began to fall as the train pulled into the station. We could see the Americans inside the lighted train cars, pressing their faces to the windows, looking out at us with exhaustion, confusion and joy.

We waited for the train to stop so that we could greet them, welcome them, show them the city we had helped build, ask them about Duluth and its big, foggy lake and green hills, and tell them our history, how we came to be here and why we came, so long ago. As the train stopped before us with a long shudder and a screeching of brakes, we waited in the rain to take the American visitors to our Russian homes.

Afterword

In the fall of 1990, after spending a year teaching and writing in the United States, I returned to the Soviet Union to find the country in shambles. Lines for food and consumer goods were longer than they had been in years, and many people were doing without the most basic necessities. Yet high-ranking party officials were giving themselves pay raises and privileges left and right. After thirty years as a party member, I finally realized that the system was corrupt beyond repair. I wrote a two-page letter of resignation to the Communist party and turned in my party card.

Little more than a year later, the country fell apart for good. The Union of Soviet Socialist Republics disbanded, communism was abolished and the surviving republics formed a coalition based not on ideology but on economics.

Though the breakup clearly was inevitable, it is still hard for me to admit that the country my parents believed in so fervently and sacrificed so much for has failed. It did not fail because socialism is a bad idea, though; it failed because socialism was never practiced there. I still believe that socialism could work, given the right circumstances and the proper foundation.

Of course, in the West it is risky to call oneself a socialist. To many Westerners, "socialism" is a loaded word. But if you look around, you will see that socialism is being practiced, to varying degrees, in many Western countries.

The United States has one of the most effective volunteer movements I have ever encountered. In America, people give freely of their time and money to help others and to help society. Is that so different from the volunteer laborers of old Petrozavodsk?

And the social welfare systems in my parents' homelands—Finland, Sweden and some other Western countries—are certainly based on the same ideals my father believed in.

I believe that a country should take care of its citizens; people should take care of each other; and wealth should be distributed fairly, so that no one goes without and no one has untold riches. Whether those beliefs are called "socialism" or something else isn't important. It is the ideals that matter.

The ideals my father taught me when I was a child in Superior still ring true: Help your neighbor, be honest and true, share what you have with those who are less fortunate, and value people and cooperation above material wealth.

It breaks my heart to admit that the grand experiment of a country run by workers has failed and that our parents made a grave, fatal mistake in bringing their families here. But the motivations behind that decision are as sound as they ever were, and I will stand behind them until the day I die.

Life can only be understood backwards;
but it must be lived forwards.
Sören Kierkegaard